GOD'S DWELLING PLACE

By

John H. Essex

BIBLE STUDENT'S PRESS™

Windber, Pennsylvania

A Facsimile Project

A facsimile reprint is a photographic duplicate of the original work. We dedicate a large amount of time and resources to acquire and preserve original material, the age and condition of which have a direct effect on the outcome of our reproductions. Like the books on which we base our reprints, our copies may contain imperfections such as printing errors and flaws, as well as user markings, notations and underlining. However, we believe that these works are important enough to make available as part of our dedication in protecting, preserving and promoting valuable historical Scripture study resources. Perhaps not unlike many of the books that we re-typeset, we may not always be in full agreement with their contents.

God's Dwelling Place
by John H. Essex

Facsimile Edition

Nathan H. Pilkington
Facsimile Publication Director

ISBN: 978-1-62904-058-5

Published by
   Bible Student's Press
   An imprint of *Pilkington & Sons*
   P.O. Box 265
   Windber, PA 15963

For information on other Bible study resources,
   www.StudyShelf.com

Printed in the United States of America

TABLE OF CONTENTS

GOD'S DWELLING PLACE

Amongst the countless thousands of books on Biblical subjects there are very few indeed (if any) which deal with the subject of "God's Dwelling Place," and there is not one known to the writer which deals with the subject in the manner of this book.

The subject is surveyed in relation to the purpose of God and His ways with humanity. It shows that God was not reacting to a crisis situation in His dealings with mankind, but that the God Who planned the end also planned the beginning. The visible and temporary aspects of God's dwelling place are reviewed, from the tabernacle in the wilderness to the temples of Solomon, Zerubabel and Herod, through to the New Jerusalem. The spiritual aspects are shown to be from before the creation, through the presesnt church, until the point when death is swallowed up in victory, and God becomes All in all.

ACKNOWLEDGEMENTS

Acknowledgement is made of the studies of the late Alan Reid, and also of the late E.H. Clayton. Their research was of considerable value in preparing chapter outlines.

We are grateful to our friend Miss Hung Woon for the many unpaid hours she spent in preparing the copy for printing, and to Phil Chapman for help in preparing the covers. We are also indebted to Grace Reid, and the late Granville Walker for proof reading the final copy.

"He scatters: He gives to the drudges: His righteousness remains for the eon." (2 Cor. 9:9).

GOD'S DWELLING PLACE

PRELIMINARY THOUGHTS

It is God's desire as expressed through His apostle Paul, that we should grow into a full realization of Himself. It would, however, be impossible for us to do this unless we are given the means by which we can understand and appreciate that which is divine. To this end, He first provides us with those faculties of heart and mind that enable us to enter into this appreciation, and then gives us illustrations within the compass of our intelligence. The greatest illustration of all is, of course, His own Son, Who, as the Image of the invisible God, reveals His Father to us: "He who has seen Me has seen the Father"(John 14:9). Into the same category, but to a lesser extent, come all the types and shadows of the Hebrew Scriptures. These, in the main, direct us to Christ: "Search the Scriptures for...those are they which are testifying concerning Me"(John 5:39). But they also portray other aspects of God's character and purpose, and not least among them are the illustrations of the tabernacle and the temple, which direct our minds to a consideration of God's dwelling place.

One of the greatest desires of nearly every man is to have a home - a place that he can call his own - a place in which he can dwell permanently and securely, loved and respected by those around him. Need we then be surprised that God desires to have a permanent dwelling place? This is made clear by the aim of His purpose, as expressed in 1 Corinthians 15:28, "That God may be All in all." God desires to dwell in the hearts of all His creatures, and His permanent dwelling place is therefore universal. It is not limited to a place "made with hands" but is something infinitely larger.

"That God may be All in all" is the scriptural definition of the goal of God's purpose, the end to which all intermediate steps are pointing, the consummation to

1

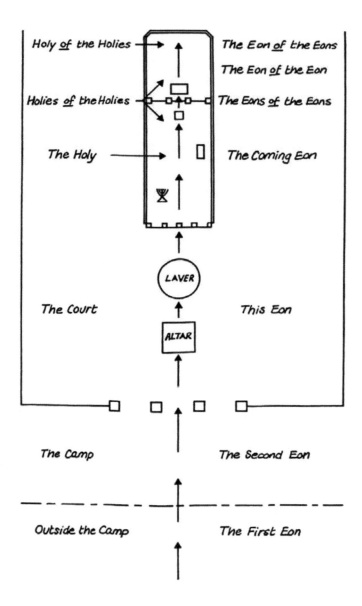

Holy of the Holies → The Eon of the Eons

The Eon of the Eon

Holies of the Holies → The Eons of the Eons

The Holy → The Coming Eon

The Court   This Eon

LAVER

ALTAR

The Camp   The Second Eon

Outside the Camp   The First Eon

which all is undeviatingly progressing. Thus we see that the theme of God's dwelling place is securely and immutably tied to that of His purpose. This being so, we can see that the theme of our study is a very important one indeed. And it has an aspect of special importance to the ecclesia of God, seeing that we are declared to be His temple (1 Cor 3:16; 2 Cor 6:16).

Our Theme Developed in Five Stages

As we come to examine the subject of God's dwelling place, we shall find that it advances in five stages, and that these cover the whole of the Scriptures and the whole of the eons.

This is not the only theme to be developed in five stages. As the accompanying chart of The Holy Places and the Eons shows, there are five stages in the tabernacle structure, and five eons which are similar in arrangement.

In each case, the first stage is a "without" stage – "without", or outside of, the camp of Israel in the case of the tabernacle, and "without", or outside of, humanity in the case of the eons (humanity was not created until the beginning of the second eon). Similarly, the first stage in the theme of God's dwelling place is a "without" stage – "without", or outside of, a dwelling place.

Again we note that the last two stages of the tabernacle structure are separated from the rest by being declared holy: the Holy and the Holy of the Holies. Similarly, the last two eons are distinguished from the rest by being associated with righteousness: the day of the Lord in which righteousness **reigns,** and the day of God in which righteousness **dwells.** These are the eons of the eons, corresponding to the holies of the holies in the tabernacle arrangement.

Such developments in five stages are not unusual in Scripture. Another parallel that readily comes to mind is the progress of the saint to resurrection glory. The first stage is "under the earth": without life; " the dead in Christ shall be rising first". The second stage is on earth: "we shall all be changed." The third stage is in

3

the atmosphere: "to meet the Lord in the air." The fourth and fifth stages take us into the heavens, first to be with Christ: "in front of our Lord Jesus, at His presence" (1 Thess.2:19; this is where we appear before the dais of Christ) and then finally "in front of our God and Father, in the presence of our Lord Jesus with all His saints" (1 Thess.3:13).

And again, with regard to the development of Abraham's seed, we find the five stages, i.e. 1. no seed (Gen.15:3), 2. Ishmael, 3. Isaac, 4. Christ, the true seed of Abraham (Gal.3:16), and 5. those of Christ Jesus, the seed by faith (Gal.3:7,29).

So, after considering the above, we shall not be surprised if we find that the first stage in the theme of God's Dwelling Place is a "without" stage, and that the last two stages have a special significance not shared by the earlier ones. And, indeed, as we shall see presently, this proves to be the case.

Briefly, then, the five stages in the development of God's dwelling place are:

1. God without a visible dwelling place
2. The tabernacle: a temporary dwelling place
3. Temples made with hands, more permanent than the tabernacle, and covering the temples of Solomon, Zerubbabel and the millennial temple as described by Ezekiel, all of which were according to God's design. (Two pseudo temples lie in between - one erected by Herod prior to Messiah's first coming, and another to be erected prior to His second coming which will be desecrated by the man of lawlessness - 2 Thess.2:4)
4. The ecclesia of God: a spiritual temple, holy and flawless in God's sight
5. God's dwelling place in spirit, leading up to His ultimate aim to be All in all

Let us now look at these stages in a little more detail, and see how they relate to each other.

4

God without a Dwelling Place

Scripturally, this covers the period from Genesis 1:1 to 16:16. During this time, God walked with Adam and Eve in the garden of Eden, but Eden provided Him with no dwelling place. He found a companion in Enoch, for it is twice recorded that Enoch walked with God (Gen.5:22,24). Noah also walked with God (Gen.6:9), but the rest of humanity became so evil that God destroyed them in the deluge. God had no dwelling place with humanity during that second eon between the disruption of Genesis 1:2 and the deluge of Genesis 7: the rebellion among the celestials which led to the disruption had ensured that He had no dwelling place among them during the first eon. And the third eon had not been long in progress before humanity again demonstrated its utter inability to provide a dwelling place for God. Instead, it sought to build a lofty dwelling place for itself, a city and a tower **to make itself a name,** but not to provide a focal point for praising God's name. Those tongues, which in the unity of a single language, should have been offering worship to God, were now confused by God in such a way as to make it even difficult for them to converse among themselves. Thus did God scatter humanity over the surface of the whole earth (Gen.11:1-9).

This "confounding", or disintegrating, of the language took away its purity for the calling on the name of Ieue, and is the exact opposite of Zephaniah 3:9. Eventually, God will reverse the process of Babel, so that all peoples may worship Him in accord, but in the meantime He brings other facets of His purpose into operation, and lays the foundation for the return of all nations to Himself by choosing a special people for Himself to be a nation of royal priests in the service of Himself and for the blessing of humanity. With this in view, He appoints a center of worship, in which the glory of His presence may reside - a tabernacle or temporary dwelling place. But before doing this, there has to be a very special revelation of Himself, and He makes this to Abram, a man whom He calls out of a land and a city of idolatry to give

5

to him the distinguished title of "father of all those who are believing."

The Tabernacle: God's Temporary Dwelling Place

The scripture in Genesis 17:1 is a most important one, for it indicates a point of demarcation, both in the method of God's operations and in the understanding and appreciation of Himself by those who would offer Him acceptable divine service. Here, for the first time, God declared Himself to be the All-Sufficient One (Heb. El Shaddai - the "Al-Who-Suffices"), and from here He began to operate in line with this declaration. All future worship of Himself must take this into account, or it would be a form of devoutness but denying its power. The evangel of the all-sufficiency of God, with its resultant blessings to all mankind, was preached in advance to Abraham, but found its full expression in the writings of Paul, which were based on the principle that "All is of God."

God's command to Abram (before his name was changed to Abraham) was that he should walk before Him, and be flawless. Note particularly, not walk with God, as Enoch and Noah had done, but before God. It was not a question of Abram being asked to assist God in what He was going to do; indeed, the last thing that Abraham was commanded to do before the birth of Isaac was to cut off part of his own flesh as a sign of his impotence to assist God in any way. Circumcision is not a badge of distinction, as many of Abraham's descendents imagined, but a sign of impotence. Now God was going to act - to set His own power into operation. He would invigorate Abram to produce the seed of His choice. He would turn him into Abraham, a father of many nations.

Further, God Himself would name the promised seed. "You shall call his name Isaac" (Gen.17:19:). No Ishmael (the son of Sarai's initiative and of Abram's own action) could stand against the claims of God's own provision. Though Ishmael might be blessed on Abraham's account (Gen.17:20), he could not inherit the blessing reserved for Isaac. Sarai's name was also changed to Sarah, by the

6

use of the same letter as was inserted in Abram's name - the fifth letter of the Hebrew alphabet. How the number five dominates Abraham's life! Called at 75 years of age (3x5x5), his son Isaac born at 100 years (4x5x5), dying at 175 years (7x5x5). And the number five was later to dominate the construction of the tabernacle. Truly, God's hand is in it all: He is operating all in accord with the counsel of His own. will, allowing no interference from outside.

Having then provided Abraham with a seed of His own choice, God further demonstrated His omnipotence and His all-sufficiency by electing a nation of His own choice. Jacob was preferred to Esau, even before they were born, and Jacob's name was also changed from Jacob (a heel) to Israel (upright with God; literally, upright with Subjector). Even in the name of the favoured nation, God emphasized His own direction as well as the status of the people. If only the nation of Israel today would recognize the significance of its name, and be subject to Him Who is its All-Sufficient-One!

As soon as the chosen people, delivered from their bondage in Egypt, began their journey to their promised land, God drew them to Sinai and made them into a nation. In so doing, He gave them His law and made His covenant with them. He also gave Moses specific directions regarding the building of a tabernacle - a sanctuary where He might meet with His people, and dwell among them (Ex.25:8). But, consistent with His being the All-Sufficient-One, **nothing in the construction of the building was left to human design or human caprice.** God's instructions regarding the building itself, and the form of worship to be maintained within it, were precise to the last detail.

Before proceeding further, let us ask ourselves,

Why a Tabernacle and Not a Temple?

When we ask a question on a matter concerning the Scriptures, there is often more than one answer, because there are so many aspects of the outworking of God's

7

purpose, and these are all interdependent upon one another. The question we have just posed is subject to more than one answer.

One reason is that God's dwelling place among His people might be mobile, so that it could accompany them throughout their wilderness wanderings, and indeed it is often referred to as "The Tabernacle in the Wilderness", in line with the scripture in Acts 7:44. But when the pattern for its design was given to Moses, the spies had not brought back their unfavourable reports of the land and its inhabitants which were the cause of the nation's lack of dependence upon God that led to the forty years' wanderings; and though we might truly maintain that God had foreknowledge of this, and made provision accordingly, this does not explain why the tabernacle was allowed to continue through all the 450 years that the judges held office in Israel (Acts 13::20). Also, if God could wait a generation when He gave the notice of the eventual temple to David, causing it to be built by Solomon, could He not have waited a generation now, and given Moses the plans for Joshua to build upon?

It also seems to be a principle running through God's purpose that the temporary comes before the permanent, and the building of the tabernacle before the temple may have been an illustration of this. But none of these considerations really gets to the root of our question, Why a tabernacle and not a temple?

Surely the answer lies in the fact that, at the time of Moses, Israel had a prophet in himself and a priest in Aaron, but no king. A king is the evidence of a kingdom and a sign of nationhood (1 Sam 8:5). A king has a settled capital, and in that capital a more permanent structure could be built. But why could not Israel have a king straight away? Why did they have to wait so long?

The answer to this is to be found in the conduct of Judah and his family back in Genesis 38, and in particular, in the twins that Tamar, his daughter-in-law, bore to him out of wedlock.

We might have wondered why this incident is recorded in so much detail in this chapter, and why it is referred to

8

obliquely in the genealogical table of Jesus Christ (Matt.1:3). The reason is that, trivial though it may have seemed, it delayed the establishment of a kingdom in Israel, and also delayed the construction of the temple. For though Jacob might prophesy that the scepter should not be withdrawn from Judah, it was to be forbidden for a bastard to enter the congregation of the Lord, even to **his tenth generation** (Deut.23:2). David was the first one of Judah's line to whom this prohibition did not apply; ten generations had passed, and he might now enter the house of the Lord. Hence his delight expressed in Psalm 122:1, "I rejoice among those saying to me, To the house of Ieue will we go". In fact, the whole of David's expression in the Psalms (Praises) is immeasurably enhanced by the knowledge that the obstacle to his family entering the house of God has now been removed; hence his frequent reference to the house of God (house of Ieue) in the Psalms (e.g., Psa. 23:6; 26:8; 27:4 and many others). David is the first one of the house of Judah who could have written the Psalms, and his delight in being able to "dwell in the house of the Lord" is expressed throughout, and is only matched by his desire to build the Lord a permanent house in which He could dwell. As we well know, this desire was not fulfilled by David himself, though he made extensive preparations towards the project. The actual construction was begun and completed by Solomon.

Solomon

Reference to the genealogical table of Jesus brings to mind two other incidents which have a direct bearing on our subject, and perhaps it would be most convenient to deal with them now.

The first is the reference in the table to "the wife of Uriah" (Matt.1:6). This, of course, reminds us of David's great sin, recorded in 2 Samuel 11. It might be considered strange that David, having perceived and enjoyed the lifting of the prohibition on his family, should so quickly run the risk of having it reimposed for a further ten generations through his illicit union with Bathsheba, but it only shows the pressures to which David

9

was subjected by the Adversary, for we have no doubt that Satan engineered the incident, even as we feel sure that he was behind the threat to destroy David physically through Goliath. If David could be destroyed;, then all the promises centered in him would be brought to nought; the newly formed kingdom would be brought into disrepute, and God's purpose would be thwarted. Now Satan attacked David on a moral issue, and David failed, but God saw to it that the child born out of wedlock did not survive. Solomon was afterwards born in wedlock, for David took Bathsheba as his wife after the death of Uriah, and it is specifically stated that the Lord loved Solomon when he was born (2 Sam.12:24), just as, centuries earlier, He had loved Jacob in preference to Esau (Rom.9:13), and had loved Israel above the surrounding nations (Deut.7:6-8). This preferential love of God is, in each case, aligned to His purpose at the time.

Though God showed His great displeasure at the conduct of David concerning Bathsheba and Uriah, there was nothing to stand in the way of Solomon building God's temple.

Zerubbabel

The other incident in the genealogical table is the begettal of Zerubbabel by Shalthiel (Matt.1:12). This is significant because both Shalthiel and Zerubbabel are also mentioned in Luke's genealogical table (Luke 3:27), though Luke gives all the names in reverse order to that of Matthew.

Both of these tables show the lineage of Jesus Christ, and from David onwards, the lines separate. Matthew gives the regal descent through Solomon; Luke gives a line of legal descent through Nathan, the second surviving son of David and Bathsheba. Twice this second line breaks; once when Neri has no son, and his daughter marries Shalthiel, and then when Heli (Eli) has no son, and his daughter Mary (Miriam) marries Joseph. In each case, the law of Numbers 27:8 goes into operation, and the father's inheritance passes to the daughter.

10

The need for the second line through Nathan was because the legality of the first line through Solomon was broken by God in his judgement against Coniah (Jeconiah), when he declared that none of his seed should ever sit on the throne of David (Jer.22:29,30). From the moment that this judgement was given, any descendant of David through Solomon, to have any regal rights, must be able to trace a legal descent through another channel from David. This Jesus was able to do because of the two lines of descent coming together in Joseph and Miriam. But, as we have just seen, they had previously been brought together in Shalthiel and the daughter of Neri, which meant that Zerubbabel had similar rights, though he was never actually made king because of the prophecy of Ezekiel 21:26,27. The question remains, why did the lines of descent come together at this point? We suggest that the answer is, so that there should be a regal representative of David present when the new temple was constructed. (Incidently, it gave an almost immediate indication how God would overcome the effects of the curse on Coniah, and fulfil His declaration of Jeremiah 23:5).

Zerubbabel was made "Governor" of Judah by Cyrus, but there is no doubt that, in God's sight, he was the regal successor of David. The temple was to be rebuilt; Israel had a prophet in Haggai and a priest in Joshua, but where was the regal representative? Zerubbabel (whose name occurs 25 times, 5x5, in scripture) was God's answer to this question.

If we have still any doubts as to the status of Zerubbabel in the eyes of God, let us read what is said about him in the prophecies of Haggai and Zechariah (Hag. 2; Zech.4). These clearly associate him with the building of the temple, and show him as a picture of Messiah.

Can we now dispute that God is the All-Sufficient-One, operating all according to the counsel of His will, even to the most minute detail, as is evidenced in His control over the lives of those mentioned in these genealogical tables? The more we read, the more we marvel at His greatness, until we sing with David, "Great is the Lord, and greatly to be praised" (Great is Ieue, and being praised exceedingly).

11

In this spirit, we hope to continue in further articles, the subject of His dwelling place.

A further example of development in five stages concerns those who are called according to God's purpose (Rom.8:28 - 30), who are:

1. Foreknown: when without existence, except in the mind of God.

2. Predesignated while chosen in Christ, before the disruption of the world (Eph.1).

3. Called: while in the flesh, like Saul of Tarsus.

4. Justified: made righteous - holy and flawless in God's sight.

5. Glorified: conformed to the body of Christ's glory (Phil.3:21).

Chapter Two

THE TABERNACLE IN THE WILDERNESS

THE TABERNACLE, or tent of meeting, which God caused to be erected after He had formed Israel into a nation at Sinai and had entered into covenant relationship with them, was the first sanctuary which He authorized and as such is worthy of study as being a pattern for subsequent divine dwelling places.

We have already noted its temporary nature and referred to the fact that the temporary often precedes the more permanent. For just as Abraham, Isaac and Jacob, the fathers of Israel, had dwelt in tabernacles because, by faith, they waited for "the city having foundations, whose Artificer and Architect is God" (Heb 11:9,10), so God provided His people with a temporary meeting place while they waited until He authorized the building of a temple with foundations. In passing, and jumping forward many centuries, it is perhaps not without significance that Paul was by trade a "tentmaker", for he regarded any earthly dwelling as temporary while he awaited a more permanent residence, "a building of God, a house not made by hands, eonian, in the heavens" (2 Cor.5:1).

But before we come to the actual construction of the tabernacle, let us briefly look at some of the events which occurred immediately prior to, and during, its authorization.

A Song of Praise

God had successfully led His people out of Egypt and delivered them from the power of their tyrannical masters. He had destroyed the authority of Pharaoh; the horse (symbol of conquest) and its rider (the defiant warrior) He had thrown into the sea. Moses and the children of Israel had sung the song of deliverance as described for us in Exodus 15, "I will sing unto the Lord [Ieue].... He is my God, and I will prepare Him a habitation; my father's God, and I will exalt Him."

13

This is an individual song (as shown by the use of the pronoun "I") sung by the people unto the Lord, and each one undertook to prepare for God a habitation. But where is this habitation to be? There is only one place where God desires to dwell, and that is in the hearts of His own. He desires that all should sing:

> Dwell in my heart, O God;
> Let it Thy temple be,
> That songs of praise may ever rise
> Out of its depths to Thee.

This may indeed have been the thought in the minds of the singers, though, as we shall soon see, they were a long way from putting it into practice. But it is evident that they also had in mind a literal dwelling place, for verse 13 speaks of the people being guided in God's strength into His "holy habitation", while in verse 17 we have a reference to "the place, O Lord, which Thou hast made for Thee to dwell in, in the Sanctuary, O Lord, which Thy hands have established", and this is immediately followed by the Lord [Ieue] reigning "for ever and ever" (Heb. l-oulm u-od, for [the] eon and further). This is the first reference to God reigning, and also the first usage in the Scriptures of the phrase "for the eon and further", which does not appear again until the Psalms, where it occurs at least a dozen times. How significant that these terms are used in connection with the Sanctuary!

Israel's Murmurings

The children of Israel soon showed themselves to be very fickle and inconstant in their loyalty to God. In one verse they are singing a song of triumph and praise; in almost the next they are murmuring against Moses, who had led them out of Egypt (Ex.15:24; 16:2). We should not be too surprised that they murmured, though we may deplore the fact. The conditions which they found in their journeyings were very different from those from which they had just come. Many of us would sooner endure hardships

14

amidst a civilization to which we had grown accustomed than endure the privations of a comparative desert. Though God had revealed Himself to Abram as the One Who suffices, his descendants had to learn that truth by experience. The waters of Marah were most unlike the sweet waters of the Nile, being bitter and undrinkable, but God answered the complaint by making them sweet. Yet this did not stifle their murmurings for long. Having complained of thirst, they next complained of hunger, and again God was able to satisfy them, and in a way that should have demonstrated beyond any doubt that He was in full control. He gave them quails (flesh) in the evening and manna (bread) in the morning, and this manna was to continue to fall every day (excepting for the sabbaths) for forty years, until, in fact, they came to the borders of the land of Canaan (Ex.16:35).

Now it can easily be seen that this was a miracle of God's provision, but if the manna had fallen **every day**, it would soon have come to be accepted as a natural thing - as natural, for example, as the sunrise - but the fact that it fell **every day except the sabbath** and that a **double portion** fell on the day before the sabbath, maintained the truth that God Himself was personally supervising the provision. This was further demonstrated by the fact that he who gathered much had nothing over, and that he who gathered little had no lack; and still further was it demonstrated by the fact that, if anything was left over till the next day, it bred worms and stank, while that which was put in a pot, to be laid up before the Lord, kept for generations (Ex.16:14-36).

The fact that the people had to gather the manna every day was in itself a constant reminder of God's provision, yet the murmurings continued. They often took the form of a challenge against their very deliverance from Egypt (Ex.16:3; 17:3). In this, they became more reprehensible, for Moses pointed out that the complainers were not really murmuring against him and against Aaron, but against Ieue (Ex.16:8). They even complained against the manna which He provided (Num.11:4-6). Eventually their complainings on ten separate occasions were to result in their being denied an entrance into the land of promise (Num 14:22,23). Yet even this was not the end of their murmurings (see Numbers 20 & 21). Their complaining attitudes were to earn them the description of "a stubborn and contradicting people" (Isa.65:2; Rom.10:21) and were to be the subject of an entreaty by Paul, addressed to the saints of this present era (1 Cor.10:9-11). The conduct of Israel was basically no different from the conduct of humanity as a whole, and what happened to them was written for our admonition. Let us then take heed of what the apostle says, and be doing all without murmurings and reasonings, that we may become blameless and artless, children of God, flawless, in the midst of a generation crooked and perverse (Phil.2:14,15). Then shall we appear as luminaries in the world.

Yet it was among this people, stubborn, contentious and contradictory, that God proposed to dwell, and it was this same people whom God purposed to establish as a peculiar treasure to Himself - a kingdom of priests and a holy nation, to minister to the world as a whole, and to pass on His blessings to all mankind. It was for this reason that He made a covenant with them before Sinai and gave them His law. They promised to obey God's voice and keep His covenant. But God did not speak with them direct - only through His servant Moses, who was called to the top of the mount while the rest of the people were not allowed to touch even the edge of its lower slopes (Ex.19).

Sin, the Barrier

It is clear from this that in spite of their covenant relationship there was a barrier between God and His people - a barrier which prevented the people from having free access to Him, and which precluded Him from having an unrestricted dwelling place among them. That barrier was sin - the sin of the people, which (as we have seen) manifested itself from time to time in murmurings, and which showed itself in all its hideousness and enormity when Moses was up the mount, receiving the ordinances which they had promised to obey. Alarmed by his long absence, they persuaded Aaron to fashion a golden calf, which they

16

claimed to be the representation of the gods which brought them up out of the land of Egypt.

In this worship of a golden calf, the Israelites were reverting to the adoration of an Egyptian idol, Apis, who was always portrayed in this form and was supposed to represent the powers of nature. Such a form of worship was in complete disregard of the second commandment, which expressly forbade the construction of graven images. By their action the people were denying God the glory that was His as the great Deliverer of the Israelites from the power of Pharaoh - a deliverance which was to be cited over and over again in the Hebrew Scriptures as a criterion of God's might. Worse still, they were (to use the words of Paul) changing the glory of the incorruptible God into the likeness of an image of a corruptible quadruped (cf Rom.1:23). In all this, they demonstrated the need for cleansing procedures and atoning sacrifices before they could offer acceptable divine service.

Further, by these acts of disobedience and idolatry (including all their murmurings) the nation, designated to be a kingdom of priests to serve humanity, clearly showed themselves to be in need of a priesthood to stand between them and God, offering their sacrifices to Him, and receiving His blessings in return. Thus the stage was set for all the elaborate ritual of the tabernacle services, with the people being kept outside of the main structure, and the priests alone being permitted to enter the Holy Place, and only the chief priest being allowed inside the Holiest of all, and that only on special occasions and after proper preparation. And as Aaron had connived with the people in the construction of the golden calf, the priesthood itself needed to be cleansed before it could serve at the altar or enter the tabernacle, hence the need for the laver as well as the altar in the outer court.

The Tabernacle outside the Camp

One result of Israel's great sin in worshipping the golden calf was Moses' sudden descent from the mountain and his breaking of the tables of stone on which God had written His law.   But before this we have his impassioned plea to God that Israel might be spared from the results of His anger, for God had actually suggested that He might consume them all and make of Moses a great nation (Ex. 32: 9,10).   The advocacy of Moses put forward three great principles, which (as Moses perceived) governed God's dealings with Israel.   In fact, they apply equally to all God's operations. They are:

1. Israel was God's **possession.**   He is the **Owner of** all in heaven and earth, but of Israel in a special sense, for He brought them out of Egypt (Ex.32:11).
2. **God's own glory** was involved in the preservation of His peop!e. He cannot cast them off (Ex.32:11,12; Rom.11:1). Similarly, for His own glory's sake, God cannot abandon any part of His purpose, but must pursue it to its ultimate.   If for no other reason than His own glory, God must eventually be All in all.
3. **God must fulfill His promises** (Ex.32:13). He cannot lie; He cannot be unfaithful, He cannot disown Himself (cf 2 Tim.2:13).

A further consequence of Israel's sin was that God declared that He would not go personally with them, but would send a messenger before them (Ex.33:2,3).   As a result of this, Moses took a tent and pitched it well outside of the camp, and called it the Tabernacle of the Congregation (literally, the Tent of Meeting), after the name that God had given to the real Tabernacle yet to be built.   Thus it came about that those who sought the Lord had to seek Him outside of the camp.   How far removed was this from the concept of God's dwelling place within the hearts of His people!

God had withdrawn Himself.   In the face of corporate failure to give Him the glory that is His due, this is what inevitably happens.   It is equally true in our own day.   Because of the general conduct of humanity in that "knowing God, not as God do they glorify or thank Him", God withdraws Himself from them and gives them over (three times) to uncleanness, to dishonourable passions, and to a

disqualified mind (cf Rom.1:21,24,26,28).   Yet, outside of
the camp of fleshly humanity, God's Spirit dwells in the
hearts of those who are His (Rom.8:9; 1 Cor.3:16;).

In this tent of meeting, outside of the camp of Israel,
God continued to talk with Moses, that servant who was
faithful in all His house (Heb.3:2), and it was there that
God, in response to Moses' pleadings, reversed His decision, and said, "My presence shall go with thee, and I
will give thee rest" (Ex.33:14).   As a result of Moses'
intercession, God was to show Himself to Israel as "Ieue,
Ieue Alueim, merciful and gracious, long-suffering and
abundant in goodness and truth" (Ex.34:6).   He would
replace the broken tables of stone and would accept
offerings towards the construction of the tabernacle to be
placed in the midst of the people.

The Design of the Tabernacle

Let us now remind ourselves of the design and layout of
the tabernacle structure, approaching it as from the outside, and not in the way in which God presented the details to Moses.   We stress again that nothing in these
arrangements was left to human choice or planning, but God
stipulated every detail both in regard to the structure
itself and to its contents.   In so doing, was not God
setting the pattern for the whole of His purpose, culminating in that grand and glorious dwelling place that shall
embrace all His creatures?   Is He not "operating all in
accord with the counsel of His will" (Eph.1:11)?   And when
He is ultimately All in all, will not all creation be,
like His temple of today, the ecclesia, "His
achievement" (Eph.2:10) ?

First of all, then, in the tabernacle structure, there
was the outer court, rectangular in shape, its length
being 100 cubits and its breadth 50 cubits.   Its height
was five cubits (Ex.27:18).   (Various suggestions as to
the length of the cubit have been given, ranging from 17
to 25 inches, or up to 63 centimeters.   This, however, is
not material in this context: what is important is that we
should note the Hebrew measurements, and in particular the
repetition of the number five and its multiples in almost

19

all the measurements of the tabernacle). The only entrance to the court was at the eastern end and was 20 cubits wide (Ex.27:16). Between the entrance to the court and the tabernacle itself were placed the altar and the laver, in that order. The altar was a square of 5 cubits and was three cubits high (Ex.27:1). The measurements of the laver are not given (Ex.30:17-21).

The tabernacle itself stood towards the western end of the court and was also rectangular in shape, its sides being 30 cubits and its ends 10 cubits. It was also 10 cubits high; that is twice the height of the perimeter of the court, so that it could be seen from outside. The first, or eastern, part of the structure was an oblong, 20 cubits by 10 cubits: this was the Holy Place. The western part – the Most Holy Place, or the Holy of the Holies – was a perfect cube, 10 cubits long by 10 cubits wide by 10 cubits high.

The tabernacle was entered, again at the eastern end, through a curtain into the Holy Place; this was separated from the Holy of the Holies by another curtain, or veil.

The Holy Place contained three items; a table of show-bread on the north side, a sevenfold candlestick on the south side, and an altar of incense just before the veil. The Holy of the Holies had only one composite item of furniture – the Ark of the Testimony (Ex.25:22). This was a chest of shittim wood, overlaid with pure gold; its golden lid formed the mercy seat, or propitiatory – this had a cherub at each end (Ex.27:1-9). The place of God's meeting with His people was thus defined exactly: "I will commune with thee from above the mercy seat, from between the two cherubims which are upon the ark of the testimony, of all things which I will give thee in commandment unto the children of Israel" (Ex.25:22).

It must be appreciated that the order in which we have described the parts of the Tabernacle is the order in which they are approached by the chief priest in his pro-gress from the camp of Israel to the presence of God in the Holy of the Holies. It is not the order in which God described their construction. On the contrary, God began by giving Moses directions concerning the Ark, and then followed with the description of the table of showbread and the golden candlestick before giving instructions regarding the tent itself. In other words, God went straight to the heart of the matter - He began by fixing the place where He Himself was to be found, and then put the coverings and barriers around. This was to be no open dwelling place, but one concealed behind curtains, only to be reached by special permission and after obeying specific instructions.

God's Longing

The provision of the tabernacle demonstrated God's desire to dwell among the people of His choice. This yearning of His heart was vividly expressed in the phrase, "That I may dwell among them" (Ex.25:8 & 29:43-46). He wanted to be among them because He loved them (Deut.7:6-8; Jer.31:3,4). The intensity of God's love will always keep alive His longings to dwell among those whom He loves, and this will manifest itself more and more until ultimately it triumphs over every obstacle and He becomes All in all.

Yet though in the tabernacle God may be said to have dwelt in the midst of His people, His actual contact with them was, as we have seen, far removed. For an ordinary person to enter into His presence meant instant death; for an unauthorized person to offer incense on the altar before the veil also meant death. Prescribed procedures had to be followed meticulously. Even the chief priest could die if he failed to observe the requisite formalities (Ex.30:19-21). How remote is this initial stage of God's dwelling among His people from His ultimate, when He will be All in all! Indeed, how far removed it is from the present position, when we, being justified by faith, may be having peace toward God, through our Lord Jesus Christ, through Whom we have the access also, by faith, into this grace in which we stand. For through Christ we have the access, in one spirit, to the Father (cf Rom.5:1,2; Eph.2:18). What a privilege is ours!

******

21

The tabernacle in the wilderness was eventually completed in accord with the specifications which had been given by God to Moses, and the day came for its setting up, as described in the last chapter of Exodus. There we read "So Moses finished the work. Then a cloud covered the tent of the congregation, and **the glory of the Lord filled the tabernacle**"; (Ex.40:33,34).

A wonderful point is to be noted here. The tabernacle was constructed by human hands, but the glory of the Lord could fill the accomplished work because it had been done in accord with His directions. It is fair to suppose that had one iota been changed to satisfy human caprice God would not have blessed the whole with His presence. No, the tabernacle was from start to finish the work of God; humans were only His instruments, operating according to His will. Hence the God of their fathers was able to dwell in the sanctuary which they had prepared for Him.

To anticipate, for the moment, later studies, and to carry the analogy into the present day, our hearts can only be the dwelling places of God if we recognize that the temples we think we have prepared for Him are, in fact, **His** achievement, created in Christ Jesus for good works, which God has prepared beforehand that we should be walking in them (Eph.2:10).

God Endows His Servants

It is further of great interest to note that, not only had God given full directions as to how the tabernacle and its contents were to be constructed, but He had also endowed certain ones with special gifts to enable them to undertake the work. In particular, Bezaleel, the son of Uri, the son of Hur, of the tribe of Judah, had been "filled with the spirit of God, in wisdom and in understanding, and in knowledge and in all manner of workmanship, to devise cunning works, to work in gold and in silver, and in brass, and in cutting of stones, to set them, and in carving of timber, to work in all manner of workmanship" (Ex.31:2-4). Others, described as "wise hearted", had likewise been filled with the spirit of

22

wisdom to accomplish whatever God desired (Ex.28:3; 31:6; 36:1-5).

Again, looking to the present era, can we not see the significance of Paul's prayers for us in Ephesians? "That the God of our Lord Jesus Christ, the Father of glory, may be giving you a spirit of wisdom and revelation in the realization of Him, the eyes of your heart having been enlightened, for you to **perceive** what is the expectation of His calling, and what the riches of the glory of the enjoyment of His allotment among the saints, and what the transcendent greatness of His power for us who are believing, in accord with the operation of the might of His strength..." and "that you, having been rooted and grounded in love, should be **strong to grasp**, together with all the saints, what is the breadth and length and depth and height - to know the love of Christ as well which transcends knowledge - that you may be completed for the entire complement of God". That same spirit, which had operated in those early chosen servants to accomplish that which God had desired, the building of His dwelling place, assuredly operates in us to the same end, for we read in another place, "it is God Who is operating in you to will as well as to work **for the sake of His delight**" (Eph.1:17- 19; Eph.3:17-19; Phil.2:13).

Another feature that was prominent in the construction of the tabernacle was the **voluntary** nature of the work. Whatever had been required had to come in the form of a willing gift - an offering to the Lord from whoever was of a willing heart (Ex.25:2; 35:5). When Moses had appealed for gifts, the people had brought over and above what was required, so that they eventually had to be restrained, and it had all been done so willingly (Ex.35:29; 36:1-7). It is clear from Exodus 36:2 that it was God Who had operated in them, even as He now does in us, to will as well as to work for the sake of His delight.

God's Leadings

Wherever the children of Israel went, the tabernacle went too, and whenever they camped, the tabernacle was set up in their midst. Or rather, let us put it another way:

23

whenever God desired the people to move, the cloud - the outward, visible manifestation of His presence - was lifted from the tabernacle, ready to move away. Then the camp was quickly broken up and the people followed the cloud until it stopped in a new resting place, where they again pitched their tents. Thus throughout their wilderness experience, the people had a Divine leader, and the cloud by day and the appearance of fire by night assured them of His presence with them.

God is just as much with us today - indeed, even more so - though we do not need **visible** signs of His presence such as were granted to the Twelve at Pentecost. No, visible signs are appropriate for those still in flesh, looking with physical eyes; we are not in flesh, but in spirit, if so be that the **spirit of God** is dwelling in us (Rom.8:9). This evidence of God's presence corresponds to His glory **inside** the tabernacle, not visible to those outside, for He Who shone with such brilliance inside the Sanctuary is He Who shines in our hearts with a view to the illumination of the knowledge of His own glory in the face of Jesus Christ (2 Cor.4:6).

With regard to the taking down, and the transporting, and the setting up of the tabernacle each time a move was made, God's directions were again most specific. Certain ones had certain duties to be performed in a certain order; these are outlined for us in the early chapters of the book of Numbers (especially Num.1:50-2:34; chapter 4 and 10:11-28). Whenever the tabernacle was set up, three tribes encamped on each of its four sides; thus the structure was always pitched in the midst of the people, signifying that God's dwelling place must always be at the center, or heart, of matters. Here it was situated at the center of a multitude of His chosen people; later it would be centered in the individual hearts of His chosen ones; in the ultimate it would be fixed for ever in the hearts of all His subjects.

In respect to the tabernacle, a great point to be noted is, that from the moment of its first erection, the life of the people and the order of their movements were always required to be related to the presence of God and the

24

position of His Sanctuary among them. This principle could only be violated at the nation's peril.

Although we are considering the tabernacle as God's dwelling place, let us for a few moments diverge from our main theme in order to glance at the offerings which needed to be made by the people before they could receive of the blessings that emanated from the sanctuary.

These are described in the early chapters of the book of Leviticus, and were of two kinds: those which, when burnt upon the altar, arose as a sweet savour to God, and those which gave off a savour which was not sweet to God. In the first category were the burnt, meal and peace offerings; in the second were the sin and trespass offerings. (Note: "Meal" offering is a better translation than "meat" offering, used in some versions.) These two categories are clearly differentiated in such scriptures as Psalm 40:6 and Hebrews 10:5,6, the latter a quotation from the former.

All these offerings undoubtedly picture Christ in His crucifixion experience; indeed, the two scriptures just referred to clearly connect them to Him, when they quote Him as saying, "Lo! I am arriving - in the summary of the scroll it is written concerning Me - to do Thy will, O God."

Offerings in the first category have as their characteristic, **willing service** - notice the phrase in Leviticus 1:3, "He shall offer it of his **own voluntary will**". Such offerings give off an odour that is pleasing in the extreme to God, and they found their fullest expression in the voluntary acceptance by Christ of the will of God, so poignantly declared in Gethsemane, which made Him "obedient unto death, even the death of the cross" (Phil.2:8). That same disposition which was in Christ Jesus may also be in the saints today, causing them to "present their bodies a sacrifice, living, holy, well pleasing to God" (Rom.12:1).

Offerings in the second category, seeing that they are dealing with sins and offences, have as their characteristics, deliverance and conciliation. To effect these results (partial in the case of the typical sacrifices, complete and permanent in the case of Christ) the unblemished must be sacrificed for that which is blemished, the One without sin for the sinner, the righteous One for the offender. These offerings point to Christ alone; His sacrifice was all-sufficient to deal with sin itself, thus allowing God to become the Justifier of the one who is of the faith of Jesus, and it was sufficient to deal with trespasses (offenses), thus allowing Him to be at once conciliated to His creation.

These two categories of offerings are clearly portrayed in the crucifixion of Christ, which lasted for six hours and took place in two stages. During the first three hours, Christ was the burnt offering (and the meal offering and the peace offering); during this stage, He could talk to His Father, and in fact did so. But in the second three hours, He was the sin offering (and the trespass offering), and during this time His Father turned away from Him. Only when the light returned at the end of this time could He cry out in anguish, "Eloi, Eloi, why didst Thou forsake Me?"

The Meaning of the Darkness

The darkness which surrounded the cross is highly significant; and if we have moved away from the tabernacle for a moment, it is because the Levitical offerings, though foreshadowing what was to occur, could never quite measure up to it. In other words, just as the shedding of the blood of bulls and of goats could never actually take away sin, neither could the offerings taken into the tabernacle quite match up to what they were intended to portray. For when, throughout all the years that the tabernacle (and later the temple) sacrifices were in operation, did God turn away from an offering? When did it become dark in the midst of the sacrificing? On the cross it became dark at noonday, just when by natural laws it should have been brightest.

Why did it become dark at the cross? It is not sufficient to say, "Because Christ was a sin-offering, although He undoubtedly was just that, as Hebrews 10 makes abundantly clear. No, there was more to it than that. The statement in 2 Corinthians 5:21 defines the position more exactly when it says, "For the One not knowing sin, He [God] makes to be sin for our sakes, that we may be becoming God's righteousness in Him."

In some versions, the word "offering" occurs after the word "sin" in this passage, though in the CV it is put in lightface type in order to show that it may be left out if desired.

The true contrasts of the passage are as tabulated here:

(a) The One not knowing sin
  (b) He makes to be
    (c) sin
      (d) for our sakes
(a) that we (sinners)
  (b) may be becoming
    (c) God's righteousness
      (d) in Him.

Set out like this, we perceive a connection in every section, and the contrast in (c) is between sin, in the absolute, on the one hand, and God's righteousness, in the absolute, on the other.

Paul is not only telling us here that Christ became a sin-offering for our sakes, but is also expressing something much more basic; that He, the One not knowing sin, was made to be the personification of Sin itself, so that Sin, in its entirety, could be crucified - destroyed for all time. When we see that sin means "missing the mark", we can see how this completely brings down the one barrier that exists between God and His people, and makes both justification and conciliation possible.

It was because Christ became Sin that God turned away from Him (not merely because He was a sin-offcring). This is the meaning of the darkness which surrounded the cross at noonday. This was what Jesus perceived in Gethsemane, that He, the sinless Son of God, was to be made to be Sin, and thus become abhorrent to God. And His own Father was to do this to Him! This explains the intensity of His agony in the garden, and the depth of feeling behind His cry, "My Father, if it is possible, let this cup pass from Me". It also shows the completeness of His acquiescence in His Father's will when He immediately added, without any hesitation, "However, not as I will, but as Thou" (Matt.26:39; Mark 14:36; Luke 22:42). Thus did He show His obedience unto death, even the death of the cross. Luke's account, in particular, gives a graphic description of the agony through which He went at this time, when it speaks of His sweat falling to the ground as if clots of blood.

The Effect of the Cross

We have dealt with this matter in some detail because we see the death of Christ, in which He was temporarily, yet completely, alienated from God, as the event in God's operations which enables Him to dwell in the hearts of His individual subjects, whom He now admits to a relationship of sonship. Israel, **as a nation,** was His son, His first- born (Ex.4:22), and, as a composite nation of twelve tribes, He could dwell **among them,** even in their midst. But **personally** they could only obtain access to His sanctuary through His, and their, representative, the high priest, and that only once a year, on the day of atonement, after the offerings had been made. Then the high priest was able to act as an intermediary, presenting the people's offerings to God, and afterwards emerging from the sanctuary to bring God's blessings to them.

But even this arrangement, though lasting for many years, was not to go on without interruption. Because of the **national** idolatry, which erupted from time to time, God would withdraw His presence, sometimes allowing His dwelling-place to be destroyed. In spite of their more durable materials of construction, the temples erected by Solomon and Zerubbabel both eventually suffered in this way. How different is this from the state of those whom God now recognizes as His temple! Those, in whom He now deigns to dwell, may count upon that indwelling as a state of permanence. This is because of the justification and conciliation which He has brought about through Christ's death on the cross, when the One not knowing sin was made **to be** sin for our sakes, that we may be becoming God's righteousness in Him.

28

Additional Note

The number "five", which we came across so often when we were looking at the structure of the tabernacle, comes again to the fore in the offerings and services connected with it.

As we have seen, the gracious work of Christ as our Saviour is typified by five different offerings in the book of Leviticus, three of which were sweet savour offerings and two non-sweet savour offerings. The choice of sacrifice for the burnt offering lay among five different creatures, of which three were animals and two were birds (bullock, sheep, goat, turtledove, pigeon - Leviticus 1).

The holy anointing oil, used to sanctify the priests, the tabernacle itself and all its furniture, had five ingredients, of which four were spices and one, olive oil. The spices (myrrh, sweet cinnamon, sweet calamus and cassia) were all taken in quantities which were multiples of 25, or five times five (Ex.30:23-25).

Chapter Three

THE ARK OF THE TESTIMONY

In our considerations so far, we have seen how God dwelt in the midst of His people, in the Tabernacle which He had caused them to construct to His design. The actual location of His presence among them was clearly defined in Exodus 25:21,22 and Isaiah 37:16 as being "between the cherubim" which were upon the ark of the testimony in the Most Holy Place.

Because of its supreme importance as the focal point of God's presence in this original dwelling place, we should perhaps give some time to a consideration of the ark.

It was called "the ark of the testimony" (or covenant) because it was made to contain the tables of stone which Moses brought down from the mountain (Deut.10:1-5), and which were the evidence of the covenant which God had made with Israel at Horeb (or Sinai) - see Exodus 25:16, 21; 34:29; 40:20; Hebrews 9:4. God's presence with Israel was established upon the firm basis of the covenant which He had made with them, but the fact that this was a covenant of law, which required observance of the people, meant that God's presence could be withdrawn if the people did not keep their side of the commitment. This, in fact, was later to happen.

Contents of the Ark

In addition to the tables of stone, upon which were written the ten commandments of the law, two other items were kept inside the ark. These were the pot of manna, which God commanded to be preserved (Ex.16:33-35; Heb.9:4) and Aaron's staff which germinated (Num. 17:10; Heb.9:4). These, too, are significant.

The pot of manna was a testimony to God's ability to provide, and also to His faithfulness in maintaining that provision. Although there was apparently little or nothing growing in the wilderness to sustain a large number of people over a long time, God was more than equal to the occasion, and they never lacked for food. Throughout the nation's forty years of wandering, the manna fell from heaven, day after day without fail, except for the sabbaths, which were covered by a double portion falling on the previous day.

Aaron's rod or staff, which germinated, and in one night brought forth buds and then blossoms and then almonds, was another witness to the power and faithfulness of God. It came about in answer to a rebellion against those whom God had appointed as His representatives (Numbers 16), and God commanded that it be kept "for a token against the rebels" and (God added), "thou shalt quite take their murmurings from Me, that they die not" (Num.17:10).

It is clear from later Scriptures that both the pot of manna and the staff that germinated were representative of Christ. He declared Himself to be "the true Bread out of heaven" (John 6:32), and He is also the One that turns away indignation and brings about conciliation from God. Aaron's rod had previously turned into a serpent before Pharaoh (Ex.7:10), and had consumed the serpents of the wise men of Egypt. The serpent is a symbol of sin (missing the mark); Christ was made to be sin for our sakes, and, in this way, destroyed sin and opened the way to deliverance and life. The almond tree, bursting earliest into flower and fruit, is called in Hebrew "the waker" - what a beautiful picture is this of Christ, the Firstfruit of them that repose! See also the lovely illustration of the almond rod in Jeremiah 1:11,12, where, after the prophet had declared that he saw the rod (or stick) of an almond tree, God said, "Thou hast well seen, for I will hasten My word to perform it" (CV: "I will be alert over My word, to do it").

The rebellion of Korah and those with him is typical of the rebellion of humanity as a whole. Korah opposed the jurisdiction of Moses and Aaron, and therefore rebelled against those whom God had set up. The earth opened to devour them. Humanity rebelled against God, and was returned to the soil from whence

31

it came, equally surely, if not quite so dramatically.
Nevertheless, it is recorded that the sons of Korah
perished not, and their descendants were later appointed to services in connection with the temple.
Some of the Psalms are associated with them.*   And
just as there were those of rebellious Korah who would
be privileged to serve God in this way, so there will
be those out of humanity who are saved from the general indignation falling upon mankind as a whole, to
be given a standing even more closely associated with
God's dwelling place, as were the sons of Korah. For
of such it is declared that they "belong to God's
family" and "are being built together for God's dwelling place, in spirit" (Eph.2:20,22).

Significance of the Ark

If the contents of the ark illustrate Christ, what
are we to say about the ark itself? The more we examine it, the more we see how it points us to Him, and
there are many beautiful lessons to be learned from a
close inspection of it, both in its composition and
its subsequent history.

Firstly, it was made of two materials, shittim wood
overlaid with pure gold (Ex.37:1,2). This represents
His humanity, overlaid with that which likens Him to
God, so that even in His human form He could still
say, "He who has seen Me has seen the Father" (John
14:9). The mercy-seat (propitiatory) on top of the ark
was also of pure gold (Ex.37:6). Christ Himself is
described as "a Propitiatory" in Romans 3:25 (see also
Heb.2:17). It is clear that, whatever purpose was
served by the propitiatory in the tabernacle is fulfilled in even greater measure by Christ. In the tab-

* The Concordant Version of the Psalms is being published in
installments in "Unsearchable Riches" magazine, published by the
Concordant Publishing Concern, 15570 Knochaven Rd., Santa Clarita,
CA 91350, USA.

ernacle, the sins of the people were covered for a year, but not eliminated (Heb.10:4), by the sprinkling of the blood of bulls and he-goats upon the propitiatory; but the death of Christ truly does eliminate sin, and thus ensures a deliverance which leads into nothing less than complete justification of the one who is of the faith of Jesus. The law, placed inside the ark, is indicative of Christ's ability to keep it - it was the whole law and not the broken one. In that prophetic utterance by David in Psalm 40:6-8, which clearly refers to Christ (for the passage is quoted, and related to Him, in Hebrews 10:5-7), it is declared that God's law is within His heart. He, in fact, was the only One able to keep it: the One without sin.

The ark was to be regarded as sacred and holy. No unauthorized person was allowed to look into it or to touch it (Num.4:15). We remember the divine judgement which befell the men of Bethshemesh "because they had looked into the ark of the Lord" (1 Sam.6:19), and also the judgement upon Uzzah, who mistakenly put out his hand to steady it (2 Sam.6:6,7). Regarding Himself, Jesus declared, "No one is recognizing the Son except the Father (Matt.11:27; Luke 10:22), and again, "No one can be coming to Me if it should not be given him of the Father" (John 6:65). There was, too, a moment in Christ's experiences when no one was allowed to touch Him - that was before He had ascended to His Father to present the true Offering of which the typical offerings were only pictures (John 20:17). Afterwards, He allowed Himself to be handled freely (John 20:27; Luke 24:39).

Whenever Israel moved from one place to another in their wilderness journeys, the ark was carried in front of the people by the Levites, and when the time came for them to enter the land of promise, it led the way into the river of death (Jordan), and held up the water on either side so that the people could pass through dry-shod (Joshua 3). "When ye see the ark... go after it," commanded Joshua's officers (v.3). Centuries later, Jesus was to present Himself to John at this very same stream, and be baptized into it, signi-

fying His subsequent baptism into death. His followers are exhorted to be "looking off to the
Inaugurator and Perfecter of faith, Who, for the joy
lying before Him, endures a cross, despising the
shame..." (Heb.12:2).

One further reference to the movements of the ark
is of special interest. There was one occasion when
it was deserted by the Israelites, and allowed to fall
into the hands of their enemies. Indeed, it was even
placed in a pagan temple. Nevertheless, it discom-
fited those who held it, and toppled and broke in
pieces the pagan god (1 Sam.4 and 5). Likewise there
was an occasion when Jesus was forsaken by all His
followers (Mark 14:50). This was when He had been
betrayed into the hand of His enemies, and though He
appeared to be completely in their power when He was
nailed to the cross, nevertheless, by refusing to worship the one whose hour it was, He vanquished them all
in His death, including him who has the might of
death, even the Adversary (Heb.2:14). Indeed, far from
being defeated, "He must be reigning until He should
be placing all His enemies under His feet. The last
enemy is being abolished: death" (1 Cor 15:25,26; cf 2
Tim.1:10).

The Cherubim

One feature of the ark that is particularly striking is its lid, made of gold, with a cherub at either
end, all of one piece (Ex.25:17-22). The cherubs are
looking inwards, so that they appear to be gazing upon
the blood which is sprinkled annually on the lid (the
propitiatory), from which, because they are part of
the same block of metal, they can never be separated.
The cherubs have wings, which overspread the propitiatory and meet above it.

Considerable speculation as to the meaning of
these, and other, cherubs (usually called cherubim in
the plural) has been offered from time to time, and
the Scriptures themselves are not too explicit. The
word means "living creature", and is so described in

34

Ezekiel 1, where the prophet is given a vision of four of them (it is made clear in Ezekiel 10:20 that these were cherubim). We have them again in Revelation 4:6, where they are in the centre of the throne and round the throne of God. There we read that "they have no rest day and night, saying, "Holy! holy! holy! Lord God Almighty, Who wast and Who art and Who art coming!"

When one desires to establish the scriptural meaning of a word or phrase, it is usually helpful to go back to its first usage, and examine it carefully. The first occurrence of **cherubim** is in Genesis 3:24, when at least two of them were placed at the gate of the garden of Eden "to keep the way of the tree of the living". On this occasion, they were accompanied by a flaming sword which was turning itself.

Here it is clear that they are associated with judgement. Adam had disobeyed God, and was forbidden the tree of life in consequence. The cherubim barred the way, for they were God's agents, representing His righteousness and justice and integrity.

In an article in **Unsearchable Riches** (Vol.36, page 32), Bro. E. H. Clayton wrote, "The presence of the cherubim indicates coming judgement. In Ezekiel they are beneath the throne, whilst in the Unveiling they are incorporated into the throne. The first mention of them in Genesis 3:24 employs them to guard the way to the tree of life, and in the holy of holies, over-shadowing the lid of the ark containing the law, we see their zeal and concern for God's law. In the tabernacle and temple they are much in evidence, being almost a centre of the service, possibly reminding of the divine presence therein, and the importance of the law and worship."

Judgement is not always condemnatory. There is no flaming sword above the propitiatory; rather, the protective wings of the cherubs would seem to prevent this. They are looking down at the blood, and are assured that the justice of God is being satisfied.

All this is pointing us again to the work of Christ. In Him the law was fulfilled, and, in accept-

ing His offering as that of the One without sin Who
was made to be sin for us, God provided a way of deliverance through faith in His blood. In former times
God spoke to His people from between the cherubim, and
His forbearance allowed Him to pass over the penal-
ties of sins. Now He speaks to us in a Son, and His
absolute righteousness is not in any way offended by
His justifying of the one who is of the faith of
Jesus. God is completely propitiated in His Son; He
is conciliated, and there is nothing on His side to
prevent creation receiving from His hand the blessings that come with reconciliation.

The Cherubim applaud the Lambkin

All of God's purpose is centred in Christ, and all
His promises are Yes and Amen in Him. In the Book of
the Unveiling of Jesus Christ, there is a beautiful
picture of first despair and then rejoicing. The
fifth chapter begins with a vision of the One sitting
in heaven upon a throne, with a scroll in His right
hand, and a cry goes up, "Who is worthy to open the
scroll and to loose its seals?" And the record goes
on, "And no one in heaven nor yet on earth, nor yet
underneath the earth, was able to open the scroll,
neither to look at it."

It appeared that there was not one in the whole
universe worthy to perform this function, and John
lamented much. But then one of the elders said to
him, "Do not lament! He conquers! The Lion out of
the tribe of Judah, the Root of David, is to open the
scroll and to loose its seven seals!" And then John
continues, "And I perceived, in the centre of the
throne and of the four animals (the cherubim)...a
Lambkin standing as though slain...." And when It
took the scroll, the four animals (the cherubim)
joined with the twenty-four elders in singing a new
song, extolling the virtues of the Lambkin. This song
progressively gains strength as others join in the
chorus, first thousands of messengers around the
throne (Rev.5:11,12) and finally "every creature which

is in heaven and on the earth and underneath the earth and on the sea, and all in them" (v.13). And after this great paean of praise has resounded through the universe, the four animals (the cherubim) say, "Amen!" They are in complete accord with what is occurring, and testify to their satisfaction.

A Retrospect

But now let us go back for a moment to man's expulsion from Eden and note an interesting point. Genesis 2:8 tells us that the garden had been planted "in the east", and therefore it would seem that any immediate expansion of the garden would have been westward. But Adam and Eve were expelled in an eastward direction since (as we have seen) the cherubim and flaming sword barring access to the tree of life were at the end of the garden.

Now it is a fact that, in the Scriptures, progression from east to west is an indication of God's favour, while movement from west to east is often a sign of disfavour. In Ezekiel's prophecy, when the glory of the Lord departs from His house, it goes towards the east, and when it returns it comes from the east (Ezek.10:18,19; 43:2). The tabernacle, too, was always erected to face the east, so that the high priest, walking through from the court to the most holy place, proceeded from east to west.

The sun appears to cross the heavens from east to west, bringing with it the blessings associated with daylight. The second presence of Christ is likened to the lightning which is coming out from the east and is appearing as far as the west (Matt.24:27). The star, which guided the magi at the time of His first coming, travelled from east to west.

Abraham's journey from Ur of the Chaldees to Canaan was (as the crow flies) from east to west; so, too, were Paul's missionary journeys, and with them the consequent spread of the evangel. It is not without significance that the most exalted of all Paul's writings, the prison epistles, were written in Rome, the most westerly point of his recorded travels. Nor is it without significance that the subsequent direction of the evangel has been generally westward – to countries like Germany, Switzerland, Britain and America.

Banishment from God's favour is, however, in an easterly direction. Adam and Eve went eastward out of Eden; Cain went eastward to the land of Nod (Gen. 4:16); Lot journeyed east when he pitched his tent toward Sodom (Gen.13:11,12); both Israel and Judah were carried eastward when they went into captivity to Assyria and Babylon respectively.

At the time of their expulsion, Adam and Eve seemed to have little in which to rejoice. True, they could approach God at the entrance to the garden, but the cherubim and the flaming sword prevented any further advance. The way to life was closed, effectively and completely, and would not be reopened until He, for Whom humanity had been created, and Who was to come in the likeness of humanity, would open the way by His death on the cross. "I am the Way and the Truth and the Life" said Jesus. "No one is coming to the Father except through Me" (John 14:6).

The inspired record in Genesis 3:24 states that God "is driving out the human, and is causing him to tabernacle at the east of the garden of Eden" (CV). It would appear that God regarded man's expulsion from Eden as temporary, and subsequent revelation confirms this, even though it would be several thousand years before Edenic conditions would be restored in the new earth. We must remember that time with God is not as we count time, for "one day is with the Lord as a thousand years and a thousand years as one day" (2 Pet 3:8). God is not tardy as to His promises nor as to His purpose, but works out His supreme will in His own time and way. Meanwhile, Adam's tabernacling literally to the east of the garden typifies humanity's tabernacling in a figurative sense to the east of God's favour. In the tabernacle in the wilderness, God gave evidence of His intention to provide a way by which humanity might be restored to favour, though permanent peace could not be established until after

38

the scene on Golgotha. The annual walk of the chief priest from east to west into the holy of holies, bearing the blood of the atoning sacrifice, was a constant reminder of God's will, and a pointer to Christ, in Whom all God's purpose is accomplished.

The wanderings of the children of Israel prior to their entrance into the land of promise were in every direction - north, south, east and west - and apparently most haphazard, as a map will show. This is typical of the wanderings of humanity as a whole groping about in a spiritual wilderness, and not seeming to know where it is going. Yet God was leading Israel all the way, and eventually brought them to a point opposite Jericho, and just above the Dead Sea, where they could cross Jordan in an east-west direction to enter Canaan. In the same way, wandering humanity (though unaware of God's leadings) is being inexorably brought by the One Who is operating all according to the counsel of His will, to the point where the only passage to salvation and peace is through the blood of Christ.

No matter what the children of Israel did, and however neglectful they were, God's purpose was not to be changed. Though they might allow the very focal point of God's dwelling place - the ark itself - to fall into alien hands, it would still be found in its rightful place when the temple was eventually built. Then the omer of manna and Aaron's germinating rod would be missing, for if the temple of Solomon is to prefigure the more permanent millennial house of the Lord (as Solomon's reign prefigures the millennial rule of Christ), then it must pre-suppose a time when the true Bread from Heaven (typified by the manna) would have been given for the life of the world (John 6:47-51), and the Firstfruit (typified by the almond rod) would have been roused from among the dead. But so long as rule and authority exist, law must remain as the basis of Divine judgement, for out of Zion shall go forth the law, and the word of the Lord from Jerusalem. And although humanity as a whole allows that which the ark portrays, Him in Whom God delights, to be given up to His enemies, and even concurs in the crucifying of the Lord of glory, nevertheless God, Whose mercy toward them that fear Him is so great that He would remove their transgressions from them, as far as the east is from the west, will still pursue His purpose to the uttermost, for He will make even the fury of humanity to acclaim Him (Psa.76:10, CV). He is the living God, Who wills that all mankind be saved and come into a realization of the truth (1 Tim.2:4).

Chapter Four

SOLOMON'S TEMPLE

In our studies thus far, we have given considerable attention to the tabernacle in the wilderness, as this was the first of three structures about which God gave directions as to how they were to be built, and was therefore a kind of prototype. Not that the temple of Solomon, on Mount Moriah, and the still future millennial temple described by Ezekiel, are replicas of the tabernacle in every detail - far from this; yet clearly principles and patterns were established in the tabernacle which are carried over into the later constructions, as we shall see as we come to examine them.

David's Desire

When King David's throne was firmly established and his kingdom was at peace, he turned his thoughts towards the building of a permanent temple in which the ark of the Lord could be housed (1 Chron.17:1). No doubt his zeal was encouraged by virtue of the removal of the prohibition on his family which we discussed in our first study - a prohibition which had prevented his ancestors from entering the house of God. David was indeed glad and rejoiced among those saying to him, "To the house of Ieue will we go! (Psa.122:1).

David's love for God's house is expressed in many of the Psalms, but particularly in Psalm 26:8, "Ieue, I love the pleasantness of Thy house, and the place of the tabernacle of Thy glory". He rightly associated the dwelling place of God with the ark, which he had recently housed in a tent in his own city, Zion, following its recovery from its alien lodgings (see the succession of events as recorded in 1 Chron.13:3; 2 Sam.6:12), and 1 Chron.16:1).

David had shown great regard for the ark of God. He had brought it into his city with gladness (2 Sam. 6:12), and he saw that a daily ministry was performed before it (1 Chron.16:37). He had composed a wonderful

Psalm of Thanksgiving after its safe arrival in Zion (1 Chron.16:7-36; Psa.105). But now he expressed his further misgivings to the prophet Nathan. "See now, I dwell in a house of cedar*, but the ark of God dwelleth within curtains" (2 Sam.7:2).

Though God approved of David's longing, David himself was not allowed to build the new structure; that task was to be given to his son Solomon. David was forbidden to undertake the work because he had been a warrior and had shed much blood upon the earth (1 Chron.22:8). Nevertheless, he received the pattern of the whole concept from God, and this he passed on to Solomon (1 Chron.28:11-13). David also did much of the preparatory work, as we read in 1 Chronicles 22. In addition, he purchased the site on which the temple was to be built. The circumstances leading up to this purchase are remarkable.

The Site of the Temple

In the time of Moses, the people of Israel had been numbered by God's command, and each had been required to give an offering unto the Lord "as a ransom for his soul, that there might be no plague among them" (Ex. 30:12). The money collected (from the people thus redeemed) was used for the service of the tabernacle (v.16).

Now when David, many years later, decided to number the people, he did it, not at God's command, but under the provocation of the Adversary, and for his own gratification (1 Chron.21:1,2). He was not considering them as God's people, but as his own, when he made this decision. He soon came to recognize his action as a sin, and as a direct result God sent a pestilence upon Israel which destroyed seventy thousand men

---

*Cedar is a wood that is never attacked by worms, and is almost incorruptible. It is therefore extremely durable. David's house was built of cedar, and God would give instructions for this wood to be used extensively in the construction of His temple.

(v.14). But when the pestilence reached Jerusalem, God suddenly halted it, and said to the destroying messenger, "It is enough! Now slack your hand". And we read that the messenger at that moment stood by the threshing floor of Ornan, the Jebusite (v.15).

At this precise spot where the plague was stopped, David (under God's direction) erected an altar. To do this, he first purchased, at full value, the threshing floor of Ornan (also called Araunah), together with oxen for sacrifice, and threshing and other instruments for fuel, the whole costing **fifty shekels of silver**. This is according to the account in 2 Samuel 24:18-25. But when we come to the account in 1 Chronicles 21:18-30, we find that David gave to Ornan **six hundred shekels of gold** by weight, which is infinitely more than the price paid for the actual threshing floor. The gold that David gave to Ornan secured the rights to the far greater area surrounding the threshing floor - the place on which the temple (with its courts and other buildings) would eventually be erected (2 Chron.3:1,2),

It is significant that the altar was constructed and the temple was built at the very point where the plague was stayed. The place where judgement was stopped and grace was manifested, was truly a suitable site for the worship of God. The spot on which David erected his altar was purchased with **silver** - silver being the emblem of redemption - but only **gold**, symbolic of Divine glory, could be given to purchase the site of the temple - God's dwelling place.

This actual site of the temple was within the confines of Mount Moriah (2 Chron.3:1), the "mount of the Lord", the place where Abraham had been directed to build an altar on which to offer his own son in sacrifice (Gen.22:2). It is the place which Abraham called "Ieue-jireh", meaning, "In the mount of Ieue it is being seen". It is quite clear from all that we have been learning about it, that it is a sacred place, specifically chosen by God.

The Foundation of the Temple

The stones, which formed the base of Solomon's temple, were very big (1 Kings 7:10), and they still remain, closely joined, firm and immovable. Yet that which was built upon them - the temples of Solomon, Zerubbabel and Herod have all gone, and part of the site is now occupied by a Moslem place of worship, the Mosque of Omar, sometimes called "the Dome of the Rock". It is another instance of the basic truth that God's foundation remains secure, no matter what may be built thereon (cf.2 Tim.2:19 and 1 Cor.3:10,11).

The temple of Solomon lasted about 400 years; that of Zerubbabel about 500, and that of Herod only about 90 years. How long will the Mosque of Omar be permitted to remain on the sacred site? It has already occupied it for more than thirteen hundred years, but that does not make it more permanent than its predecessors. At some point of time, it must give way for the future temple to be constructed.

The Glory of the Temple

The glory of Solomon's temple lay not so much in its size - that of Herod was to be infinitely greater - as in its magnificence. The value of the gold and silver accumulated for it by David (1 Chron.22:14) has been estimated to be worth, in today's currencies, about two thousand million dollars or one thousand million pounds. Be that as it may, there is no doubt that the splendour of Solomon's temple excelled the splendour of any other buildings of its time, and probably of any other building since. It was God' building, and He provided His servants with all that was required to make it one of extreme glory.

It is clear from 1 Chronicles 28:11-19 that the pattern of the temple, which God gave to David, showed that building to be more complex than the earlier tabernacle. There were additional chambers and courts, suited to a permanent structure, which had been missing from the temporary, portable one. It is not our

purpose to go into the details of the temple construction, for that would extend these chapters into an in-
ordinate and unacceptable length. Rather, we would
select points which seem to us to have special spiritual significance. Suffice it to say for the moment
that the difference between the simplicity of the
tabernacle in the wilderness and the glory of the
temple of Solomon was as marked as the difference between Christ in His fleshly tabernacle, and Christ in
His resurrection glory. If we can think of Christ in
the flesh as a temple in which God delighted to dwell,
as He surely was (John 14:10,11), how more glorious
should we regard the risen Christ, in Whom, "the entire complement of the Deity is dwelling bodily", and,
indeed, "delights to dwell" (Col.2:9; 1:19).

The Holy of Holies

Essential to both the tabernacle and the temple was
the most holy place - the holy of holies - the actual
dwelling place of God. The difference between the
sacred chamber in the tabernacle and that in the temple was that the latter was eight times the size of
the former. Both were perfect cubes, but whereas the
most holy place in the tabernacle was 10 cubits long
by 10 cubits wide by 10 cubits high (making a volume
of 1,000 cubic cubits) that in the temple was 20 cubits long by 20 cubits wide by 20 cubits high (making
8,000 cubic cubits, cf 1 Kings 6:20).

The important thing to note is that in each case
the length, breadth and height are equal, thus forming
a perfect cube. In the temple God enlarges His dwelling place in all directions by doubling the measurements. But this enlargement, though significant, is
small compared with what we find when we come to the
new Jerusalem, in which God eventually tabernacles
among mankind; for the length and breadth and height
of the holy city are again equal, but are very, very
much greater than the measurements of His earlier
dwelling places within the tabernacle and the temple
(cf Rev.21:16). And greater still are the dimensions

of God's dwelling place in spirit, spoken of in Ephesians 2:22, for this has "breadth and length and depth and height" beyond finite measurement and indeed almost beyond comprehension (Eph.3:18), since this embraces all in the heavens as well as all on the earth, and envisages God's ultimate of being "All in all".

But coming back to the holy of holies in the temple, we have noted that this is eight times the size of the corresponding place within the tabernacle. Number in Scripture is often very significant, and Dr. Bullinger says that "seven means that which is spiritually complete or satisfying, eight denotes that which is superabundant or satiating" (Number in Scripture, p.196). In concordant Hebrew, "eight" belongs to the word family oil, with such variants as fertile and stout.

How true is this in connection with Solomon! He was granted wisdom beyond measure and riches so superabundant that the Queen of Sheba, when she visited him and saw the glory of his kingdom, was compelled to exclaim that "the half had not been told her", and Solomon himself gave in superabundance, more than ever she requested (1 Kings 10:1-13). In this, he portrays God Himself.

Solomon and the Queen of Sheba

To Solomon, with regal pomp surrounded
And matchless wealth, the Queen of Sheba came.
His glory she would see and prove his fame
Which through her own dominion had resounded.

Soon her most lasting doubts were all confounded;
For though reports had once seemed overbold,
She owned that fully half had not been told
As each new vision left her more astounded.
Then did the king, according to his pleasure,
Bestow rich gifts upon his honoured guest,
And from the vastness of his royal treasure,
Above what she desired, he chose the best.
Thus, too, gives God in more abundant measure
Than ever His recipients request.

The Enlarging of God's Dwelling Place

The most holy place in Solomon's temple, enlarged eight times when compared with its prototype in the tabernacle, is truly in line with the idea of super-abundance; for if that which is of the tabernacle points to Christ while in the flesh, then that which is of the temple is truly illustrative of Christ in resurrection glory. And even while He was in the flesh, but looking forward into the future, Jesus said, "I came that they might have life eonian, and have it superabundantly" (John 10:10).

Once the point of Golgotha is reached in God's purpose - the point at which the plague of sin is effectively halted - then the way is open for life eonian to be enjoyed in superabundance. That which was typified by the pot of manna has been given for the world, and that which was typified by Aaron's rod has been accomplished in the rousing of Christ, the Firstfruit. These emblems are no longer hidden within the ark, as they were in the tabernacle. That which they illustrate - the death and resurrection of Christ - are now widely known facts of history, hence are absent from a temple prefiguring the dwelling place of God in the next eon. The death and resurrection of Christ lead Israel directly into Messiah's Kingdom blessings.

The continuing enlargement of the place in which God dwells runs parallel to the progressive enlargement of His work in Christ. In the next eon, life is given to those who obey the rules of the Kingdom, so that one who dies at a hundred years old is as a youth and made light of (Isa.65:20). In the last eon when the new Jerusalem becomes a fact on earth and God tabernacles with mankind, life as humanity first knew it is fully restored. Death and all that accompanies it will be no more; nor will there be any more doom. The spring of the water of life will be given gratuitously and a tree of life will be rendering its fruitage continuously - not once a year, as is customary with trees now, but twelve times a year (cf Rev.21:1-6; 22:1-3).

Life will then be freely available to all on earth, but even this is not the ultimate. The heavens are not yet brought into the picture, nor is there any mention (in the Book of the Unveiling of Jesus Christ) of vivification or immortality. These come only within the still wider concept of Paul's evangel, based upon an understanding of Christ's sacrifice that accords with God's own multifarious wisdom and His absolute righteousness. In this understanding, the One not knowing sin is seen to have been made to be Sin, as we pointed out in our third study.

It is in the complete destruction of sin on the cross of Christ that God can so enlarge the confines of His dwelling place that they do not remain confines at all, but spread out to include all in heaven as well as all on earth, for it is through the blood of Christ's cross that peace is made and universal reconciliation effected.

The building of the temple at the place where the pestilence was stayed is just a picture of what God would be able to achieve when once the plague of sin is halted. No wonder that the temple of Solomon was glorious! But infinitely more glorious will be the outcome of all God's achievement in Christ, for then He will be All in all.

God's Word must be fulfilled. "In the mount of Ieue it will be seen.

Chapter Five

THE MUSIC OF THE TEMPLE

There is one feature, absent from the Tabernacle services, which was greatly in evidence in the temple worship, and that is music.

Music in scripture is generally associated with joy and thanksgiving. It may take the form of singing and the playing of instruments, and is sometimes accompanied by dancing (cf Exodus 15:1, 20,21). By singing, we do not necessarily mean pitching the voice on different notes, as is commonly understood today. When Moses sang his song to the Lord, it is recorded that he "spoke, saying ..." (Ex.15:1). There can be true music in the spoken word when that word is truth; true praise can emanate from lips unable to do more than croak if the heart is in tune with God, just as true prayers can ascend to God when the suppliant is too broken to utter more than "inarticulate groanings" (Rom.8:26). Let us always remember that

> 'Tis not the harmony of sound
> That pleases most the ear Divine,
> But when a trusting heart is found
> To be, O Lord, in tune with Thine.

Music as a form of Praise

Music finds its noblest expression when it resounds in praise to God. As such it is often spontaneous, as when singers give vent to their joy at the realization of a divine accomplishment, or at the reception of especially good tidings. We see this intuitive reaction in the response of those celestial beings who were present when the earth was founded, for we read that all the stars of the morning joined in jubilation, and the sons of the Alueim expressed their feelings with a shout of acclaim (Job 38:7). It was also evident in the sudden assembling of messengers giving praise

to God for the birth of a Saviour; it needed only one
messenger to announce the glad tidings to the shep-
herds, but it required a multitude to give adequate
and immediate praise to God (Luke 2:8-14). It will be
especially evident again when, as described in Revelation 5, One is found worthy to open and read the
scroll which had been seen on the right hand of the
Supreme Occupant of the throne in heaven. Notice how,
in this case, the paean of praise swells, in three
distinct stages, until it eventually includes "every
creature which is in heaven and on the earth and underneath the earth and on the sea, and all in them".
What a tremendous outpouring of praise that will be!

The spontaneity already mentioned is again seen in
the singing by Moses and the children of Israel of
their song of praise to God as they stood on the safe
side of the sea after seeing their Egyptian pursuers
overwhelmed. We find the full song in Exodus 15, and
we noted in an earlier study that one of its ingredients was the desire of the singers to prepare for
God a habitation (**Unsearchable Riches**, March 1976,
page 52).

Miriam magnifies God with her Music

So joyous an occasion was this deliverance from the
bondage of Egypt that Miriam, the sister of Moses,
took up the song just sung by her brother, and gave it
additional emphasis by leading forth all the women in
an accompaniment of timbrels and dancing (v.21).

Miriam is mentioned only a few times in scripture,
and not always to her advantage, but she was the one
who watched over the infant Moses, even as her name-
sake in the Greek Scriptures was to watch over the
infant Jesus (Miriam and Mary are the same name in
different languages). But Miriam is called a prophet-
ess - the first woman to be so described in God's Word
- and she is specially mentioned in Micah 6:4 where
God says, after recounting how He brought Israel out
of Egypt, that He sent before them "Moses, Aaron and
Miriam."

Thus, hundreds of years after they had all died in the wilderness, God remembers these three persons - not Moses and Aaron only, but Miriam as well. He had given them to Israel, and though all three had failed to such an extent that none was allowed to enter the land of promise, yet God recalls their names with loving regard for their service to His people. He forgets their sins but remembers their service, and, by drawing Israel's attention to them, shows that He places a value on that service. In other places, He declares that Moses was faithful in all His house (Num.12:7; Heb.3:2).

Miriam took a timbrel (tambourine), and led the women in playing and dancing. They provided the music, an essential part of the praising of God, as David (perhaps with Miriam in mind) makes clear in Psalm 149:3 and in the whole of Psalm 150 - note the first clause in verse 4. Alas that after the dancing of Miriam and her companions, the next recorded instance of such dancing should be to a golden calf (Ex. 32:19)! Such however was the fickleness and inherent perversity of Israel, symptomatic of the general instability of all mankind.

Miriam praised God by her singing and playing. Centuries later, other Miriams would come forward to glorify God by their actions in regard to His Son - in His conception (Luke 1:46), in His death (John 19:25), for the day of His burial (John 12:3-5), and in His resurrection (John 20:11-18). Truly the name has been perpetuated in honoured service.

Although musical instruments are first mentioned in Genesis 4:21, the original Miriam is the first one of whom it is recorded that she used a musical instrument in praise of God. Moreover, the song in Exodus 15 is the first mention of singing as events are recorded in the Scriptures. By the time of David, both playing and singing were to have a great part in the worship of God. How often does David say in the Psalms (Praises), "O Sing to the Lord". He takes the music into the dwelling place of God, even as we are entreated to do today. We are to be filled full with spirit, speaking to ourselves in psalms and hymns and spiritual songs, singing and playing music in our hearts to the Lord, giving thanks always for all things, in the name of our Lord, Jesus Christ, to our God and Father - in psalms, in hymns, in spiritual songs, singing, with grace in our hearts to God (Eph. 5:19-21; Col.3:16). God, in the person of His Son, should be dwelling in our hearts - his spirit should also be making its home in us - and there, into our hearts, the temple of God, we should be taking the music of thanksgiving, for whenever we thank God, we magnify Him as the great and all-sufficient Provider and Sustainer.

The opposite of singing is murmuring. When things do not appear to be going well with us, the natural tendency of the flesh is to complain. Like Israel of old, we tend to grumble at the least provocation. But Paul entreats us to "be doing all without murmurings and reasonings" (Phil.2:14), for only in loyal and unselfish devotion to God, and complete trust in His operations, can we truly sing to Him with grace in our hearts. And indeed, if we truly believe that God is working all together for the good of those who are loving Him, and that He is ever "for us", should we not be "more than conquering" over adversity? Let us then at all times be filling our hearts with joy and praise for Him Who has not merely delivered us from the bondage of sin, great though that is, but has also justified us and given us an assurance that nothing in the whole universe can ever separate us from His vast love in Christ Jesus, our Lord (Rom.8:28-39).

The Wilderness no place for Rejoicing

In the earlier study to which we have referred, we saw how prone were the Israelites to be murmuring. The absence of Moses for just forty days was sufficient to lead them into an act of disobedience and disloyalty to God. The dancing in triumph after their deliverance from Egypt turned into an orgy of false worship to alien deities, as the people declared, "These be thy gods, O Israel, which brought thee up out of the land of Egypt". This was profanity and rebellion of the highest degree, and brought about swift judgement from God. Singing could not be resumed until this offense had been purged.

And while occasional songs were sung by Moses and the Israelites during their wilderness experience (cf Num.21:17,18 and Deut.32:1-43), there could be no real joy in their hearts while they were excluded from their promised land. The wilderness, with all its deprivations, was no place for rejoicing, and of those who commenced the journey from Egypt, only two (Caleb and Joshua) survived to cross the Jordan into Canaan.

Joy in Christ

Yes, the wilderness was indeed the place for the strewing of carcasses (Num.14:29). It is significant that, in later years, the one who was chosen to announce the ministry of Jesus is described as "The voice of one imploring, 'In the wilderness make ready the road of the Lord'" (Matt.3:3, quoting from Isa. 40:3). Though this passage is directly addressed to Israel, to whom it applies, it is nevertheless a fact that humanity as a whole had been in a wilderness environment ever since it had been turned out of the garden of Eden; its carcasses had been strewn all over the earth throughout thousands of years. It had no real cause for rejoicing; rather it was, in common with all creation, "groaning and travailing together until now" (Rom.8:22). The ministry of Jesus, confined to Israel though it was, might have seemed to offer a gleam of hope, but this appeared to have been extinguished with His death. In reality, it was this event which turned the hope into a glorious expectation. In Christ there is now the joy of salvation and the peace toward God that comes with reconciliation, and songs of praise may now be sung by those who believe, just as they were sung in the temple in Solomon's time:

Singing songs of gladness,
Favoured saints march on!
In this vale of sadness
Bid distress be gone.
Let our lips be voicing
Thanks to God above,
While we walk, rejoicing
In His perfect love.

David the Singer

David is recognized as the king who brought music
into the worship of God, though the temple was not
actually erected until the reign of his son. Many of
the Psalms are Davidic in origin, and David encouraged
the training of musicians, both in playing and singing
(1 Chron.15:16-24). Asaph, to whom about a dozen of
the Psalms are attributed, was one of these.

This was the beginning of a great era of musical
development in Israel. David probably wrote many more
Psalms than those which bear his name in the Scriptures. Solomon is credited with composing over a
thousand songs, as well as three thousand proverbs,
(1 Kings 4:32); Psalms 72 and 127 are attributed to
him. Many of the Psalms are anonymous; some of these
are thought by certain commentators to be by Hezekiah.
Where God leaves them anonymous, it is probably best
to let them remain so, but certainly Hezekiah encouraged the use of the Psalms of David and Asaph in
the house of God (cf 2 Chron.29:25-30).

The Psalms as a whole, and those of David in particular, cover the complete period of history from
creation to the time of the writers, and also include
much that was then prophetic. In general, they as-
cribe glory to God for His manifest operations, especially as concerning His people, Israel, but often
in a wider sphere, as when they speak of creation
(e.g. Psa.148:1-5) and include the heavens (19:1) and
the whole earth (24:1). There are many instances like
these.

The language of the Psalms is poetic, as can be felt from a reading of them. In the Hebrew, this is more evident than in our English translations. They are musical, as is clear from the number of occasions on which they have been set to music. They are what is now termed lyrical, for they were originally sung to the accompaniment of a lyre, or ancient harp. David himself was an accomplished harpist, for he was able to refresh King Saul with his playing (1 Sam.16:23).

David's Psalms are drawn widely from his own experiences, and do not overlook his most sinful moments, as in Psalm 51. It is truly remarkable that David's utterance, in the emotion of deep repentance, should be used by Paul in Romans 3:4 as a basic truth concerning God, to be taken as an axiom in relation to His absolute integrity. "Now let God be true, yet every man a liar, even as it is written: 'That so Thou shouldest be justified in Thy sayings, and shalt be conquering when Thou art being judged'". A further instance occurs in Romans 4:7, 8, where Paul quotes from another penitential Psalm (32) in support of his argument leading into justification.

David was a complex character. His strength lay in his reliance upon God, as when he faced Goliath. In this, and in his general concern for God's glory, he was (in spite of his lapses) a man after God's own heart, and a worthy leader of His people. And this, too, is reflected in the music of the Psalms.

A boasting challenge rang through Elah's vale,
And stunned all Israel on their mountainside.
"Send forth a man to fight", Goliath cried;
Yet none dare face that giant in massive mail
Save one slight youth,
   whose heart refused to quail.
"You come with spear and sword,"
   this lad replied,
"But in that Name, which you have long defied,
The Lord of Hosts, I come and shall prevail."
And he, who slew Goliath with a stone,
Who salvaged Israel's honour with a sling,

Was called by God to sit on Israel's throne,
The chosen forebear of earth's greatest King.
O, give me grace king David's God to own,
And like the psalmist, of His triumphs sing.

Without David's personal background, including his
time as a fugitive in the wilderness (1 Sam.23), his
Psalms would not contain the depth of feeling that is
to be found in them. They speak of trials before blessings, of dangers before safety, of sorrows before
joy. This is general experience. Lamentations may
lodge for a night, but jubilation comes with the morning (Psa.30:5). And the Psalms are speaking of God's
protection during the night, and of His deliverance in
the morning.

David has also much to say about the One greater
than himself, the coming Messiah, Whom he acclaims as
his Lord (Psa.110:1). He sees Him in His tribulations
(including even His crucifixion trials - Psa.22) and
in His glory (in the second half of the same Psalm, as
well as in others). Note the wideness of vision in
verses 27 and 28, "Remember and return to Ieue shall
all the limits of the earth, and worship before Thee
shall all the families of the nations, for Ieue's is
the kingdom, and Ruler is He among the nations."

The Songs of the Temple

What is our purpose in outlining all this? Simply
to show that the whole Word of God (as epitomized in
the Psalms) is suitable for use in God's temple. These
are the Praises, and God is indeed to be praised in
all His operations. There are few aspects of God's
purpose of which there is no hint in these songs. This
is emphasized by the number of times that the writers
of the New Testament quote from them, and not least
the apostle Paul, who does it about twenty-four times,
mostly in the book of Romans.

Music and singing were appropriate for use in connection with the reign and temple of Solomon because
they prefigure the millennial reign and temple of

Christ. The worship of the Tabernacle had been of a profound but more restricted nature, for it pointed to the sufferings of Christ; in the services of the temple we are reminded not only of the sufferings of Christ but of the glory which follows. And this is particularly true as we worship God from the temples of our own hearts. **All scripture** is for our instruction, and we should be using its teaching to fortify our spirits so that they will ever resound in praise to God.

The Psalms themselves will always be a delight to us for they form the pattern of true temple worship. They enter into every avenue of human experience as it relates to God. They are at the same time both comforting and encouraging. They tell of the response of the heart to the provision of God. Throughout they acknowledge His wisdom and His goodness. Many of their expressions are true in all eras; that is why they are so often quoted. But there are some aspects of the Psalms which need to be changed with the advancement of God's purpose. For instance, the imprecatory Psalms are hardly appropriate in this day of conciliation and grace. Even outside of the writings of Paul, the Scriptures themselves recognize the need for a new Song to conform with changing developments in God's operations (Rev.5:9).

Within the writings of Paul, there are many expressions of pure grace which form the basis of the spiritual singing which should always be rising from within our hearts. God's temples have never had such wonderful music with which to praise Him as they have today. The whole of Paul's evangel, which is indeed God's evangel concerning His Son, and is therefore the power of God for salvation, is so replete with melody that we can but say with the apostle, "Be rejoicing in the Lord always! Again, I will declare, be rejoicing!" (Phil.4:4).

57

A Crescendo of Praise

Praise should ever be increasing. Look at the Psalms themselves, and note how they rise to a crescendo of praise towards the end, and especially in the last five. They conclude with the grand statement, "Let everything that hath breath praise the Lord" ("All with breath shall praise Ie"). And then they add a personal entreaty to everyone who hears, "Praise ye the Lord". ("Praise ye Ie").

In Psalm 148 we have all the singers; in Psalm 150 we have all the instruments. Voices and instruments blend together in an increasing volume of praise that, in the end, encompasses all in earth and heaven, and this reminds us again of the expanding volume of acclamation which John hears when the One, Who is the Lion of Judah and the Root of David, takes the scroll from Him Who is on the throne.

There is a striking comparison between the vision of John in Revelation 5 and the picture that Paul places before us in 1 Corinthians 15, verses 20-28. It seems to us that one is complementary to the other. Both are comprehensive within the space of a few verses; both stretch out from a single beginning to a universal ultimate; both have an air of absolute inevitability about them. Paul's account begins with the rousing of Christ from among the dead, and from this one fact there follows a succession of events covering a long period of time (but here compressed into a few weighty sentences) leading right up to the consummation when God will be All in all. John's vision begins with the one basic fact that One is found worthy to take the scroll, and from this glorious truth the paean of praise swells inexorably until it encompasses all.

In Paul's account, the apostle concentrates on three developments, namely, the vivification of all, the subjecting of all to Christ, and the destruction of all enemies (including death), so that a completely reconciled kingdom may be handed over to God, for Him to be All in all. John's picture is of the acclaim

given first to the Lambkin and then to God by virtue
of the fact that the Lambkin was slain - this is developed in three stages (commencing at verses 8, 11 and
13 respectively) until the last one embraces every
creature in the universe. It is all so inevitable and
undeviating; in each case, it needs only one fact to
set the chain in motion; nothing then can hinder the
ultimate from coming to pass.

As we consider these things, we feel like saying
with Paul, "O, the depth of the riches and the wisdom
and the knowledge of God! How inscrutable are His
judgements, and untraceable His ways! For, who knew
the mind of the Lord? or, who became His adviser? or,
who gives to Him first, and it will be repaid Him?
seeing that out of Him and through Him and for Him is
all: to Him be glory for the eons! Amen!"

Chapter Six

DIVISION AND DESTRUCTION
(The Kingdom and the Temple)

Our Studies have so far been concentrated around the Tabernacle in the wilderness and the Temple of Solomon. Before we move on to look at later structures, let us just note the course of events which led to the ultimate destruction of Solomon's temple and see what lessons we can learn.

We saw in an earlier study that the building of this temple had to wait until the kingdom was established in Israel and the people dwelt in peace throughout the land. Also, we have suggested that the glory of Solomon's reign pictured in some measure the coming reign of Christ. Then why has not the temple been preserved for the millennium? The answer lies, not in the lack of preserving power on God's part, but rather in the unfaithfulness and idolatry of His people. (The preserving power of God is manifest in the keeping of a remnant of His people even to the present day, though they have been persecuted and scattered throughout all the earth.)

God's Warning to Solomon

God had truly sanctified His house, which He had chosen and designed, and which had been built with such magnificent splendour according to His directions. He had sanctified it and placed His name within it, as we read in 2 Chronicles 7:16.

"And now have I chosen and sanctified this house, for My name comes to be there unto the eon, and My eye and My heart come to be there all the days."

The following verses are very significant, and we quote them in full. They are addressed to Solomon.

"And you, if you will go before Me just as David, your father, went, and do according to all that I instruct you, and are keeping My statues and judgements, then will I set up the throne of your kingdom, just as I have contracted with David, your father,

60

saying, There shall not be cut off from you a man to rule in Israel.

"And if you are turning back and forsake My statutes and My instruction, which I have set before you, and go and serve other alueim and worship them, then will I pluck them off the ground which I have given them; and this house, which I have sanctified for My name, will I fling from My face and will make it a proverb and a byword among all the peoples.

"And this house, which had become supreme, will be desolated, and every one passing by it will say, Why does Ieue do thus to this land and to this house? And they will answer, Because they forsook Ieue, the Alueim of their forefathers, Who brought them forth from the land of Egypt, and because they are holding fast to other alueim and are worshipping them and serving them; therefore He brings on them all this evil."

The Warning not Heeded

From this passage of scripture, it is evident that a great burden rested upon Solomon as king of God's people and custodian of His temple – His dwelling place. In the event, we find that Solomon did the very things which God forbade (1 Kings 11). Yes, he who built the temple of God, would so demean himself as to turn to heathen gods, and build "high places" for them. In this he would lead the people astray, and would sow the seeds of that idolatry which would eventually lead to the complete fulfilment of the prophetic warning.

It may seem a matter of some astonishment that God could allow so much beautiful work to be put into a building, knowing full well that its existence would be only temporary, though it might have the appearance of permanency. Yet, when we come to reflect, we realize that God has created much, only to see it destroyed. The temple is but one of many things. Humanity itself is created but to die, and to be replaced by a new humanity, which is part of a new creation. Even heaven and earth pass away to be replaced by that same new creation, in which "the former shall not be remembered, nor shall they come upon the heart" (Isa. 65:17).

What we have to remember is that all this destruction is in line with God's purpose, and indeed is predetermined by Him. Nothing ever takes Him unawares. We cannot stress too often or too strongly that God never improvises. When, in Isaiah 46:10, He describes Himself as "telling from the beginning, the hereafter, and from aforetime, what has not yet been done", He is not ascribing to Himself some psychic or uncanny perception denied to others. No, He declares the end from the beginning because He plans the whole and accomplishes His purpose by operating all according to the counsel of His will.

This is well demonstrated in the circumstances surrounding the reigns of the first three kings of Israel, as set out in the following table. Note that each of these kings reigned for exactly forty years (Acts 13:21, 1 Kings 2:11, 11:42, 1 Chronicles 29:27, 2 Chronicles 9:30); this, in itself, is a circumstance suggesting Divine control.

Name of King	Reign	Chief characteristic	Crisis of failure	Result
Saul	40 yrs	Bodily stature	Challenge of Goliath	Rejection in favour of David
David	40 yrs	Moral strength (a man after God's heart)	Attraction of Bathsheba	War in his own family
Solomon	40 yrs	Wisdom (mental brilliance)	Lure of riches, leading to idolatry	Division of the kingdom (in the following reign)

The total testing period of 120 years (3 times 40 years) is significant. It is equivalent to the time originally given to humanity in Genesis 6:3, after which God's Spirit was taken away and all kinds of wickedness began to be revealed and to multiply. It is equivalent to the time given to Moses for him to prove a right to be the deliverer of Israel; Moses failed, and it was left to Joshua to bring the people into the land of promise. It is equivalent to the three periods of forty years, during which the land had rest under the Judges (Judg.3:11; 5:31; 8:28). After each of these, Israel immediately lapsed into idolatry, proving the unworthiness of the nation to enjoy the peace of the land. 120 years was the total time given to the kings of Israel to demonstrate their worthiness to reign over God's people. With the end of that time of probation, the kingdom would be divided, not to be reunited until He comes.

The Kingdom Promised

It should be remembered that Saul, David and Solomon were not ordinary kings. They were kings of God's choice reigning over God's people. In Exodus 19:5,6. we read of God's initial promise to the newly formed congregation of the children of Israel that, conditional upon their obedience to His voice and their keeping of His covenant, they should be not only His peculiar treasure above all people, but a kingdom of priests and a holy nation. In this promise, both the throne and the temple are indicated and connected as features of God's future operations concerning His people.

In Deuteronomy 7:6-8, God confirmed the choice of Israel as His people, and gave His reasons for the choice - not because they were more numerous than any other people, but for reasons solely dependent upon Himself: He loved them, and would keep the oath He had sworn to their fathers.

But having chosen His own people, God did not immediately appoint them a king. However, in Deuteronomy

17:14, 15, we read of how He made another reference to the possibility of a king in Israel by reserving for Himself the right to choose their king, just as He had chosen them as His people, and He expressly forbade them to choose a king from outside of their own nation.

From this pronouncement, it might have seemed that the kingdom was near, but though soon afterwards Israel entered the land of promise, around 450 years were to pass by, and still they would have no king. During that period, control was exercised by Judges (Acts 13:20).

450 years may seem a long time; to the Israelites, waiting and hoping for the establishment of their kingdom, it must surely have seemed long. But God was not idle during that period. Not once did He abandon His intention to establish a kingdom, though no signs of any activity in this direction were apparent to the children of Israel. Yet, as the book of Ruth clearly shows (and this is the purpose of that book - see chapter 4, verses 17-22), God was preserving through generation after generation that regal line from Judah which was to lead in due time to David (and Solomon, and eventually to the Lord Himself).

The First King Appointed

But the patience of the people at last gave out. In the days of Samuel they clamoured for a king, and God gave them Saul in answer to their request. With the prohibition on the tribe of Judah (referred to in earlier studies) not yet lifted, the choice of king was made from a different tribe, that of Benjamin. Saul was chosen because of his great stature and good-ly appearance; from his shoulders and upward he was higher than any of the people (1 Sam.9:2). Yes, Saul was chosen because of his outstanding physique, and when Samuel first saw him, God said, "Behold the man of whom I spoke to you. This is the restrainer among My people" (v.17).

For a short while, Saul's reign appears to have prospered, but after he had reigned about two years, he found himself rejected by God for not having kept His commandment, and Samuel, who was deputized to announce the rejection, continued with these words, "Yet now your kingdom shall not be confirmed. Ieue seeks for Himself a man in accord with His own heart, and Ieue will instruct him to be the governor over His people, for you have not observed what Ieue instructed you" (1 Sam.13:14).

Soon after this, David was anointed (1 Sam.16), but Saul remained on the throne until his forty-year testing period was fully expired; and the utter impossibility that physical qualities alone can measure up to God's requirements was demonstrated in the supreme test which was imposed upon Saul, when he was confronted with a man of outstanding physique in the ranks of his enemies. Saul, as king, and at least a head taller than any other man in Israel, should have been the one to have met the challenge of Goliath, the Philistine giant. Instead, it was left to a mere lad, unprotected by the armour which Saul would have had, and equipped only with a sling and five stones from a brook, to show how weak was the greatest strength of man compared with the power of God.

In passing, it is interesting to note that Goliath paraded before the armies of Israel exactly forty days; in other words, in this particular test, Saul was given just forty days to make up his mind to prove his worthiness by meeting the enemy of God. There is no doubt that, had Saul gone forth with the same faith in God as did David, he would have prevailed over the giant, but though his physical strength was great, his moral courage was weak. David, on the contrary, though physically small, had tremendous moral courage, based on a sure reliance on God, and this brought him triumphantly through this test. But later, when the issue was entirely a moral one, even David failed.

The Second and Third Kings

David was a man after God's own heart. We have only to read his psalms to appreciate the lovely traits of his character. It was David who wrote, in Psalm 21, "Ieue, in Thy strength is the king rejoicing! And in Thy salvation, how exceedingly is he exulting!" and, in verse 7, "For the king is trusting in Ieue and in the kindness of the Supreme; in naught will he slip" (CV). David had displayed those kingly qualities of courage and trust in God from a mere lad, yet it was David who committed that terrible crime against Uriah, thereby sinning against God.

And Solomon, the third king, failed as well. Whereas Saul was chosen for his great physical strength, and David for his moral courage, Solomon became renowned for his sheer mental brilliance, yet all his wisdom was not proof against the flattery of women and the lure of riches. In his desire for wealth, he disobeyed in several ways the strict injunctions of God (compare Deut.17:16, 17 with 1 Kings 10 and 11), and was even led into the worship of false gods, and to erect "high places" to them.

Solomon's disobedience was summed up by Nehemiah (13:26). Though "among the many nations came no king as he", yet "him did foreign wives cause to sin". Because of his disobedience to God (breaking in detail all the commands of Deut.17:16,17), the divine judgement came upon the kingdom which he ruled, and the sentence of 1 Kings 11:11 was put into effect. Nevertheless, though the kingdom was to be rent from him, verse 12 makes it clear that this was not to happen in Solomon's own time, but in the reign of his son, and we know that this took place very shortly after Solomon's death. So Solomon's reign lasted the full forty years - the time of probation, or proving, granted to him.

A similar situation would arise many centuries later when Jesus would pronounce judgement upon Jerusalem. Though her house was to be left to her desolate, and no stone of the sanctuary would be left upon a stone (Matt.23:37-39), yet it would not be till AD70 (around forty years from the commencement of Jesus' ministry) that the city and temple were actually destroyed. In the intervening period, the apostles ministered, and the kingdom was re-offered, and again rejected, in stages - first to Jerusalem and Judea, then to Samaria, and then to the limits of the land. Though we would not be too dogmatic on this point, it would seem that the kingdom had to be 'on offer' to Israel for a testing period of forty years.

The Division of the Kingdom

It is of particular consequence to note that, though God took the kingdom away from Solomon and his descendants and gave the greater part of it to Jeroboam, "the son of Nebat, an Ephratite of Zereda, Solomon's servant", He reserved one tribe (Judah) and the city of Jerusalem "which He had chosen", to form the southern kingdom, and to preserve the line of Judah and David, thus fulfilling prophecy and promise (Gen.49:10; 2 Sam.7:12-16). Although the tribe of Benjamin was also to become part of the southern kingdom (for only ten tribes were given to Jeroboam), Judah was the main tribe and the name by which this southern kingdom, centred on Jerusalem, would be called, where the site of the temple (God's dwelling place) would still remain as the focal point of God's purpose. Messiah, when He should come, would come to the holy city and to the temple; the supreme Sacrifice would take place on the holy mount - Moriah, the mountain of the Lord - the place "in which it would be seen" (Gen.22:14). And the Lord, when He comes again, will return to the same city, for "His feet shall stand in that day upon the mount of Olives, which is adjoining Jerusalem" (Zech.14:4).

Jeroboam was not a descendant of David at all; he was of the tribe of Ephraim. It is stressed that he was Solomon's servant (1 Kings 11:26; 2 Chron.13:6). One of four things that the earth cannot bear is a servant when he reigns (Prov.30:22); one of the four things which are comely in going is a king against whom there is no rising up (vs.29-31). Jeroboam was an example of the former of these; alas, Solomon was not an example of the latter. For though his reign began in peace, there were risings against him before the end, and these spoke ill for the future of the kingdom and of the temple.

The Increase in Idolatry

There is no doubt that the time we have been describing was one during which the Adversary was especially active against God and his people. Satan would know of the promises made in David; he would know, too, of God's love for Solomon, and the promises made to him. Could he thwart God's purpose by destroying the monarchy, and thus bring the kingdom to naught? His nefarious attempts seemed to have been crowned with success. Saul, David and Solomon all wilted against his attacks upon them. Solomon, in fact, became a compounder of idolatry; the kingdom was divided; the temple was doomed to eventual destruction. Idolatry among the people would soon become the rule rather than the exception, for they would follow the lead of their kings. Of the nineteen kings who were to rule the northern kingdom, all without exception would be bad, like the first one, Jeroboam, of whom it is said in scripture no less than twenty-five times that he persistently sinned and made others to sin. Of the southern kings, five (including Hezekiah) could be called good; the rest were either unstable or bad.

In an earlier study, we noted how the children of Israel had clamoured for an idol to worship while Moses was away from them on the mount, and how Aaron had built them a golden calf. Jeroboam exceeded this by building two, which he placed at opposite ends of his kingdom, so that people would have something to worship without having to travel to Jerusalem. He described them in exactly the same words that Aaron had used, "Behold your alueim, Israel, who brought you

up from the land of Egypt" (Exod.32:4; 1 Kings 12:28).
How strangely is iniquity repeated and multiplied! It
was Ieue Who had brought His people out of Egypt, and
that deliverance was a special demonstration of **His**
power, for which purpose He had even raised up
Pharaoh. Satan used Jeroboam as a tool to try to
undermine the power of God.

Nor was Rehoboam, Solomon's son, and king over the
two tribes, much better, for under him "Judah is doing
evil in the eyes of Ieue, and they are making Him jea-
lous **more than all that their forefathers did** by their
sins which they sinned" (1 Kings 14:22). This was
followed by an invasion by Shishak, king of Egypt, who
took away all the treasures from the temple and from
the king's house, after which Rehoboam made "shields
of brass" to replace the "shields of gold" which Solomon had made (1 Kings 14:25-28; 2 Chron.12:10-11).

Here we see the beginning of a deterioration, which
culminated in the destruction of the ten-tribe kingdom
(Israel) by Assyria, and the capture of Judah somewhat
later by Babylon. At the time of Nebuchadnezzar,
Jerusalem was largely destroyed and the temple completely burned by fire at the hands of aliens (Jer.
52:13).

What conclusions may we draw from all this? We suggest the following:
1. God is operating all according to the counsel
    of His will.
2. God will not be hurried by men's actions. Hav-
    ing allotted definite periods of time for cer-
    tain features of His purpose to take place
    (such as the forty years granted to each of the
    first three kings of Israel) He allows the full
    time to be worked out before He brings about
    another development. But neither does He delay,
    for once that period is worked out, events oc-
    cur swiftly as He has predicted.
3. God is ever faithful. Though the kingdom was
    divided, God does not abandon His people alto-
    gether. Though He allowed His dwelling place
    among them to be destroyed, He is still their

God. In His own due time (and not before and not after) He sent His own Son to earth as Israel's Messiah, and the Lord Whom they sought suddenly returned to His temple (Mal.3:1). This prophecy was fulfilled only in part at Christ's first advent, but will be fulfilled completely at His second coming. This, again, will be in God's own due time, neither earlier nor later. But before this, the chosen ones of the present economy - the ecclesia which is the body of Christ, will be caught up to meet the Lord in the air.

Temples may be destroyed and replaced, not once but several times, but in the present ecclesia God has a temple which will never be destroyed.

Chapter Seven

THE EDICT OF CYRUS

In our last chapter, we reached the point of the capture of Judah by Nebuchadnezzar, King of Babylon, and of the destruction of her capital city, Jerusalem, and of the burning of the temple, God's dwelling place among His people.

The land of promise, which should have been flowing with milk and honey, was left desolate, that it might enjoy the sabbaths of rest which God had ordained for it, but which the nation had failed to observe. Prophecy had envisaged this situation. The land was to be left desolate for 70 years (cf Lev.26:32-35; 2 Chron.36:21; Jer 25:8-12; Dan.9:2), a destroyed Sanctuary, a desolate Land, until the land had enjoyed her sabbaths.

A Time of Mourning

Can we not see a special significance, and an intense poignancy, in what had occurred? The temple had been built in the time of Israel's greatest prosperity, when she had been a united nation, basking in all the magnificence of Solomon's reign. The king himself had said, "But now the Lord my God hath given me rest on every side, so that there is neither adversary nor evil occurrent" (1 Kings 5:4). In the visit of the Queen of Sheba, there had been given an indication of the true position of Israel, when nations would go to her light, and kings to the brightness of her radiance (Isa.60:3). The visiting Queen had marvelled at the splendour and wisdom of Israel's king, and had been an appreciative recipient of his munificence.

But how the picture had changed! From splendour to desolation; from pre-eminence to servitude; from joy to misery and sorry.

The utter dejection of the captives is vividly portrayed in Psalm 137:1-4,

"By the streams of Babylon, there we sit.
Moreover we lament when we remember Zion.
On the oleanders in its midst we hang our harps.
For there our captors ask us for the words of a song,
And our looters for rejoicing.
'Sing to us from a song of Zion.'
How shall we sing a song of Ieue on foreign ground?"

The Jews looked back to the glories of Zion, and compared their present lot with what had been, and were utterly despondent. The contrast was extreme, and it is rendered all the more so when we consider what the name Babylon signifies.

Confusion

Babylon is the Greek form of the Hebrew word Babel, which means "confusion" or "disintegration". The orderly arrangement of divine rule, by which Israel enjoyed a position of benevolent dominance over the world in accord with her covenant title "a kingdom of priests", had been thrown into disorder, first by the breakup of the kingdom, and now by the final capture of the capital city and the utter destruction of both city and temple. Israel, because of her own idolatry and stubbornness, had proved herself to be totally unable and unworthy to serve humanity in either a kingly or a priestly capacity; now both the throne and the temple were gone. The kingdom had been taken away from the descendants of David and given to a gentile monarch, Nebuchadnezzar (Dan.2:37; 4:25).

But though God gave to Nebuchadnezzar the right to rule, He never gave him the right to be worshipped. Nebuchadnezzar did not recognize this at first and sought worship for himself through the great statue which he built. After he had been humbled by being brought down to the level of a beast, he learned his lesson, and acknowledging his mistake gave glory to God (Dan.4:36,37). Belshazzar, his successor on the throne, never learned the lesson, and when he dishonoured the sacred vessels which had been taken from the temple in Jerusalem, and appropriated them for his own carousals and praised his own material gods while drinking from them, his kingdom was taken from him and given to Darius the Mede (Dan.5).

Since the time of Nebuchadnezzar, the world has slipped farther and farther into a state of confusion, as the chaos of the present time testifies - a state, which only the coming of the Lord with power, and the restoration of Israel to her ordained status, can and will rectify. A King will reign and use intelligence (Jer.23:5), and Israel will again function as "a chosen race, a royal priesthood, a holy nation, a procured people", and will delight in recounting the virtues of Him Who calls them out of darkness into His marvellous light. They, who were once "not a people" will again be "the people of God"; they who have not enjoyed mercy will be shown mercy (1 Pet.2:9,10).

At the time of the Babylonian captivity, this was indeed a long-term view. The domination of the nations would not be ended for many centuries to come. But there would be a short-term alleviation of the position. The land was to be desolate for 70 years, enjoying its sabbaths, and then a respite would be granted. Jews would be allowed to go back to Jerusalem to rebuild their city and their temple. This was to allow the worship of God to be resumed and was in accord with the prophecy of Isaiah concerning Cyrus (Isa.44:28).

Cyrus

Cyrus, King of Persia, was truly a remarkable person. His birth was prophesied and his actual name foretold some 200 years in advance. In this he was not unique, for King Josiah's name and deeds had been foretold about 300 years before his birth (see 1 Kings 13:2 and compare it with 2 Kings 23). But Cyrus is unique in one respect; he is the only gentile to whom the term "anointed" is applied in the Hebrew Scriptures. He is also termed God's "shepherd", and God said of him, "All My desire he will perform, saying as

Jerusalem, It shall be built, and the temple, It shall be founded."

God was still zealous for the welfare of His people, even though their stubbornness had led them into captivity. The centre of Judah was Jerusalem, and the centre of Jerusalem was the temple, and the centre of the temple was the Sanctuary, the Most Holy, God's dwelling place. Though all these had been destroyed, they would be rebuilt, and Cyrus was the one appointed to issue an edict to this effect. How he did it in his first year as King of Persia is described in the book of Ezra (1:1-4).

In his studies on Isaiah, Brother E. H. Clayton wrote (Unsearchable Riches, vol. LX, page 262), "There were no possible circumstances that would hinder the return from Babylon. The water system and streams of the district and around that city were all under Ieue's control, and He was prepared to direct the one who was to carry through His intention. In fact, Ieue not only named the man who was to execute matters on His account, but He also termed him, "My shepherd". Thus does Ieue describe what He constituted Cyrus to be in respect of His people. Cyrus had to take care of Ieue's people in the same sense as the eastern shepherd had of his sheep; they are his care and protection. In his deliverance of Ieue's people, Cyrus was a type of Messiah, and would perform Ieue's desire. This was the rebuilding of Jerusalem and the founding of the temple there."

The Deity of God

Nowhere is the Deity of God more forcefully proclaimed than in the later chapters of Isaiah's prophecy, and it is remarkable that the verses which describe the unique position of Cyrus are in that sublime portion of Scripture. Look for a moment at chapter 45, the chapter which describes how God prepared the way for Cyrus in his progress to the conquest of the Babylonian empire, and declares that it was on account of His servant Jacob, and Israel, His chosen, that God had called Cyrus by name and had titled him, that is, appointed him, not just as head of the second world-wide empire (the silver of Nebuchadnezzar's dream-image) but also the shepherd of God's people. What an honour for Cyrus, yet Cyrus did not know God.

God was operating alone in His operations with Cyrus. He did not need Cyrus' help. Cyrus was but the clay in the hands of the potter (Isa.45:9). God was belting or girding him for the purpose He had in view, for He is Ieue Alueim, and there is none else, no Alueim except Him (v.5).

In verses 6-10, we have a declaration of God's supremacy in such absolute terms that they admit of no compromise. They cannot be whittled down; they must be accepted as statements of absolute truth.

> "I am Ieue Alueim, and there is none else.
> Former of light and Creator of darkness,
> Maker of good and Creator of evil.
> I, Ieue Alueim, made all of these things."

In this passage, the whole concept of good and evil is explored. God is saying, in effect, that He is responsible for the evil that has come upon Israel, just as He had indicated when He had given Jeremiah the wonderful lesson in the potter's house (Jer.18). And God introduces the illustration of the potter again in Isaiah 45:9 when He asks,

> "Will anyone contend with his Former?
> The earthenware with the ceramists?
> Is the clay saying to the potter, 'What are you making?'
> And your contrivance, 'No hands has he?'"

And then, in verse 10, God continues the argument with a double question which is very pertinent in the case of Cyrus,

> "Will anyone say to a father, 'What are you begetting?'
> Or to a woman, 'With what are you travailing?'"

75

God had named Cyrus two centuries before he came forth from his mother's womb. In those intervening years, God had been controlling the begettals and births of succeeding generations so that the right man should be born at exactly the right time. He had done the same with regard to Josiah, and was indeed controlling all the generations from David onwards, so that in due time, first the father and mother of Zerubbabel and later the father and mother of Jesus, should come together from parallel lines of descent from David, at precisely the right moment in each case for God's intentions to be accomplished. (This was discussed in more detail in our first study, see Unsearchable Riches, vol. LXVII, page 16).

Verse 13 shows God's further direction over Cyrus. He was to be roused in righteousness, and all his ways were to be straightened. He was to build God's city, and let His people go, without any thought of reward or payment. "Not for a price, and not for a bribe". Thus God exercised His power over the mightiest man in the world at that time, just as centuries before He had controlled the pharaohs of Egypt, even changing the dynasty to accommodate His purpose, so that one "not knowing Joseph" should occupy the office when the time should be ripe for God to display His power in him (Ex.1:8; 9:16; Rom.9:17). Centuries later, God would again influence the mightiest man in the world, Caesar Augustus, and cause him to pass a decree which would induce Joseph and Mary to travel to Bethlehem for Jesus to be born in the place that had been prophesied by Micah (Mic.5:2).

Nebuchadnezzar, too, had been the greatest man of his time. As God's servant (Jer.25:9), he had taken God's people into captivity. Cyrus, as God's anointed, was to shepherd them out of it.

God as a Saviour

In verse 15 (of Isaiah 45) we have a remarkable interpolation. It is as though Israel were addressing God, and saying that He was hiding Himself. Truly, He had formerly hidden Himself within the Sanctuary of the Temple, open only to the chief priest once a year, but now there was not even a temple to indicate His presence within. Where could the nation find Him? Was He still the Alueim of Israel, a Saviour?

The succeeding verses, to the end of the chapter, proceed to answer this question, and to enlarge upon it to such an extent as to show that not only Israel, but all heaven and earth, are dependent upon Him for salvation. Israel's present troubles are made to form the dark background to revelations of an infinitely wider sphere of God's operations, just as, in Paul's time, the troubles of the Corinthian ecclesia would form the backdrop for the apostle's preaching of the Word of the Cross, leading into the ultimate, "That God may be All in all."

In verse 18 it is made clear that the desolation that was encompassing Jerusalem and the land of Judea was not something that was unique. On the contrary, the whole earth had been a chaos at one time, but God had not created it so, nor did He intend it to remain so. He created it to be indwelt. If that was true of the whole earth, it was certainly true of His own land and city and temple.

The climax is reached in verses 22 and 23:

"Face to Me and be saved,
   all the limits of the earth,
For I am Al, and there is none else.
By Myself I swear.
From My mouth fares forth righteousness,
And My word shall not be recalled.
For to Me shall bow **every knee**,
And **every tongue** shall acclaim to Alueim."

These are the words of a Deity, Who, in the next chapter (v.10) describes Himself as

"Telling from the beginning, the hereafter,
And from aforetime, what has not yet been done.
Saying, 'My counsel shall be confirmed,
And all My desire will I do.'"

77

With such a God, what need had the Jews to despair? In the words of Brother Clayton again, "Creation is yet to see the glory which Ieue will achieve for His People, in spite of their tardiness to hearken and to give heed". It was essential for His glory that the city and temple should be rebuilt.

The Rebuilding of the City and Temple

Following the edict of Cyrus, a number of the leaders of Israel joined with Zerubbabel and returned to Jerusalem to begin the task of rebuilding the temple. So important was this work that the names of the families taking part in it are listed in detail in Ezra 2. They took with them the vessels from the original temple, which Nebuchadnezzar had abstracted from Jerusalem and put in the house of his gods (Ezra 1:7); these Cyrus gave back to the Jews.

But there is no mention of the ark of the covenant which seems to have disappeared, and the new temple when it was eventually completed lacked much of the glory of Solomon's. Nevertheless, it was accepted by God, and He was glorified by it (Hag.1:8).

It had not been constructed without difficulties, and there was one period of fifteen years when the work had lapsed. But it was finally completed in the sixth year of Darius the King (Ezra 6:15). The whole project had taken around 25 years.

The rebuilding of the city, and particularly of the outside walls, took much longer, owing to the hostility of surrounding tribes who had come in to occupy the land after the Jews had been taken away. Eventually, in the reign of Artaxerxes, Nehemiah obtained authority from the Persian king to go to Jerusalem, and under his direction the work was tackled diligently, the wall being finished in fifty-two days (Neh.6:15).

And so we have again a temple in Jerusalem, serving as a focal point for the worship of God. It was a witness to His people that He was still with them, as He assured them through His prophet Haggai saying, "I am

with you.... My spirit is standing in your midst. You
must not fear" (Hag.2:4,5).

The Preserving Power of God

The book of Esther, recording events that happened
about this time back in Shushan, where the king of
Persia had his summer palace, demonstrates unmistak-
ably how God was with His people, even those who had
not responded to the call to Jerusalem. Owing to the
influence which Haman, a truly wicked man who had obtained sudden advancement at the court, had upon the
king, an edict was issued which would have extermin-
ated all the Jews throughout the whole of the Medo-
Persian empire. The decrees and laws of the Medes and
Persians were supposed to be unchangeable, yet God was
able to order the circumstances around both Mordecai
and Esther so as to reverse the effect of the first
decree by the issue of a second, obtained as a result
of Esther's intercedence with the king. Thus was God
able to preserve His people and ensure the deaths of
their enemies. This deliverance is still celebrated
by the Jews at the feast of Purim, held annually in
the middle of the last month of the Jewish year.

Just in passing, it is worthy of note that the Book
of Esther provides a remarkable illustration of God
hiding Himself, for no name of the Deity is mentioned
in this account, and that makes it unique in Scripture. (It is claimed that two of the Divine names are
hidden in acrostic form within the structure of the
book, and can be traced - in the original Hebrew - in
five places.)* A careful reading of the story is
enough to show that God (though hiding Himself) was
really watching over the welfare of His people. Truly,
"neither slumbering nor sleeping is the Keeper of
Israel" (Psa.121:4).

And neither slumbering nor sleeping is the One Who
is watching over His chosen ones of today, those who

---

* See Appendix 60 in The Companion Bible.

were chosen and titled long before the disruption of the world (Eph.1:4), even as Cyrus was chosen and titled before the disruption which befell Israel at the time of Nebuchadnezzar, for are we not "aware that God is working all together for the good of those who are loving God, who are called according to the purpose that, whom He foreknew, He designates beforehand also, to be conformed to the image of His Son.... Now whom He calls, these He justifies also: now whom He justifies, these He glorifies also.... If God is for us, who is against us?" (Rom.8:28-31).

Nor is God slumbering or sleeping in respect of any part of His creation, for He "is operating all in accord with the counsel of His will" (Eph.1:11). The clarion call still goes forth, "Face to Me, and be saved, all the limits of the earth... for to Me shall bow every knee, and every tongue shall acclaim to Alueim."

Paul increases the scope of this prophecy by adding extra dimensions (height and depth) to the length and breadth of the earth, and by incorporating the name of Jesus into the picture, so that we now learn "that in the name of Jesus every knee should be bowing, celestial and terrestrial and subterranean, and every tongue should be acclaiming that Jesus Christ is Lord, for the glory of God, the Father" (Phil.2:10,11). Our God will not be satisfied, nor will His purpose be completed, until He is All in all, and until the heart of every one of His creatures has responded to the love which He has lavished upon it, and become a temple in which He can dwell, and from which He will receive for evermore the love and praise that is due to Him both as God and as Father.

Chapter Eight

THE TEMPLE OF HEROD

The temple built by Zerubbabel and his helpers lasted about 460 years before it fell into some disrepair and was renovated or rebuilt by Herod.

There are remarkable points of contrast between the temple built by Zerubbabel and that erected by Herod. The former was by God's direction, and He was glorified by it (Haggai 1:8); the latter was built by a man to serve (as Josephus says) "as an everlasting memorial" of himself. Yet the former would be desecrated by a prototype of the man of lawlessness, while the latter would be visited by the Lord of Glory, the ever obedient Son of God. In the former, an abominable idol would be erected and worshipped; in the latter, the Lord Jesus would drive out those who would desecrate the sanctuary. In the former, unclean animals would be offered for sacrifice; in the latter, an unmistakable sign would be given that God had accepted a faultless Sacrifice ("as of a flawless and unspotted lamb" - 1 Pet. 1:19), and that as a result the barrier between Himself and His creation need no longer remain. The curtain that concealed the most holy place and barred access to it, would be rent from top to bottom at the precise moment of the last act in the crucifixion of His beloved Son. For Matthew 27:50,51 makes it known that it was as Jesus "let out the spirit" that the curtain of the temple was rent.

The above is a synopsis of some of the points that we wish to develop in more detail in this particular study. We have placed them at the forefront so that we may have firmly in view the point to which we are moving - the rending of the barrier between God and His creation.

The Desecration of Zerubbabel's Temple

Zerubbabel's temple was desecrated around the year 168 B.C., nearly 350 years after it had been built. The man who defamed it was Antiochus Epiphanes.

He was a Syrian, one of the family of kings descended from Seleucus Nicator (and thereafter known as the Selucidae). His grandfather, known as Antiochus the Great, had in 204 B.C. secured control of Judea and other territories. Antiochus the Great had been harsh towards the Jews, and so had his son, Seleucus Philopater, but Antiochus Epiphanes became far harsher than both his immediate forbears. He robbed and plundered both the city of Jerusalem and the temple within it, removing the furniture from the holy of holies. He abolished the temple services, and rededicated the building to Jupiter. He massacred many of God's people and sold women and children into slavery. But his crowning affront lay in his causing unclean animals (swine) to be offered on the altar of sacrifice, and then, over this same altar, he erected a statue to Jupiter Olympus.

It is an irrevocable maxim in God's dealings with His creation that, when once something is marred, it cannot be repaired, it must be replaced by something, rebuilt or recreated. That is why there has to be a new humanity (for the old humanity was marred in Adam) and a new heavens and a new earth (for the old were marred by rebellion among the celestials, culminating in the disruption). The action of Antiochus Epiphanes made the reconstruction of the temple inevitable.

The excesses of Antiochus provoked an uprising against him, led by the Maccabeans. Mattathias, who began it, was an ageing priest, but his son, Judas, who continued and developed the revolt, became known later as Judas Maccabeus (from the Hebrew word mqbth, meaning hammer). On the ups and downs of this campaign we need not here concern ourselves, but merely note that at the end of the conflict the Jews attained a measure of independence, which they retained for about eighty years until they were engulfed within the Roman empire in 63 B.C. During this time, authority was vested in the chief priests, one of whom was John Hyrcanus, whose grand-daughter, Mariamne, later became the wife of Herod the Great. This fact is worthy of note, for later Herod was to show his hatred of her

82

family by murdering in turn her three brothers, herself, her mother and last of all her two sons which
were his own progeny. Thus all traces of the kingly-
priest line descended from the Maccabeans, were eliminated, and the way was apparently open for Herod to
assume authority in matters both temporal and spiritual. To this end, he sought first to obtain recognition from the Roman Emperor, Augustus, of the title,
"King of the Jews", and then proceeded to rebuild the
temple, thinking thus to please his subjects.

Caesar Augustus

Caesar Augustus is remembered by students of the
Scriptures as the Emperor who issued the decree that
all the world should be registered, at the time when
our Lord was about to be born (Luke 2:1). The King
James Version uses the word "taxed", but gives the
marginal rendering as "enrolled". This was not a tax-
ing of the people, but a world-wide census, for which
each one had to go to his own home city. We can imagine the consternation with which Joseph and Mary
would receive the news of this requirement, coming as
it did at a time when Mary was about to deliver her
child. There was no modern transport in those days,
and journeys were arduous and uncomfortable. Still,
the command had to be obeyed, and so Joseph undertook
the journey to David's town of Bethlehem because he
was of David's line. In other words, God made use of
the mightiest man in the world at that time and caused
him to issue a decree at just the precise moment to
accomplish the divine purpose. For Micah had prophesied centuries before that the future Ruler should
come out of Bethlehem (Mic.5:2). Certainly Augustus,
proud man that he was, and living in Rome many hundreds of miles away, never knew the real reason for
his arrogant decree.

But who was Augustus? Let us look at him for a moment. We have all heard of Julius Caesar, who con-
quered most of the civilized world of his day and even
invaded the British Isles. This was about 50 years

before the birth of Christ. If you have ever read Shakespeare's play of the same name, you will remember that Julius Caesar was afterwards assassinated in Rome, and that at his death three men came jointly into power. They were Mark Antony, Octavius (who later changed his name to Augustus) and Lepidus. For a time they ruled in harmony, Antony being master of the east, which included Egypt and Palestine, Octavius the west, and Lepidus Africa. But Octavius, by first liquidating Lepidus and then Antony, gradually assumed supreme control of the whole of the Roman Empire. He acquired in turn the headship of the army, the government and the religion, and finally he had the title conferred upon himself of Augustus, or the august one or the majestic, just as we refer to a king as his majesty.

Augustus should, however, be known to Scripture students for another reason, and that is, that, in line with God's decree through Ezekiel (21:27) that the kingdom should be "depraved, depraved, depraved" until He should come Whose right it was, he (Augustus) had actually confirmed the appointment of Herod as King of the Jews. Herod was first given this title by Antony, but when Antony was defeated by Augustus, Herod pleaded for the retention of his position. And this, according to Josephus, the Jewish historian, is what Augustus said to him, "Thou shalt be king, for thou art worthy to reign over a great many subjects. I do therefore assure thee that I will confirm the kingdom to thee by a decree."

Herod the Great

Who was Augustus to make such an appointment? God had plainly declared in Deuteronomy (17:14,15) that He Himself would choose the kings of Israel. And who indeed was Herod to accept such a position? He had not been born in Bethlehem! He was not of the tribe of Judah; indeed, he was not even an Israelite. He was a stranger, an Idumean, a descendant of Esau, who had centuries before sold his birthright to Jacob for a

84

stew. True, Herod was accepted by the Jews under compulsion as their ruler, but he was never recognized as such by God. True he built temples and palaces, and made lavish gifts in all directions, but he committed many atrocities, as when he murdered some of the Sanhedrin for their daring to point out to him that he could not be king, as he was a foreigner. The massacre of the children, described in Matthew 2, was only one affair among many crimes that he committed. How strange that Augustus, who had confirmed this monster in his office, should be made to put the final touch to God's purpose by bringing about in Bethlehem the birth of the true King!

Truly, God moves in a mysterious way, His wonders to perform! He controls the actions of the mighty as well as of the humble in order to fulfil the prophecies contained in His Word.

Prophet, Priest and King

And so we find Herod restoring the temple, and doing so in a lavish way, apparently for his own glory and to please the people, but in reality, being used of God to make sure that the temple was there to receive the true King whenever He should present Himself at its door.

We have noted in our studies in earlier chapters that with each temple there was associated a prophet, a priest and a king. This is illustrative of the threefold role which Christ Himself will play in relation to the future millennial temple, for He will be Prophet, Priest and King when He returns to earth in His glory, as the book of Revelation so aptly portrays. In the case of the tabernacle in the wilderness, the king was absent because of the prohibition still resting on the house of Judah, which was not lifted till the time of David. Nevertheless, the prophet (Moses - see Deut.18:15) and the priest (Aaron) were present. When the time for the building of the first temple arrived, the prophet was Nathan, the priest Zadok and the king Solomon (1 Kings

85

1:38-40). At the time of the second temple, the prophets were two, Haggai and Zechariah, the priest was Joshua and the regal representative of David was Zerubbabel, in whom the two lines of the genealogy from David were to meet, as they were to do again when Jesus was born.

We now come to the temple of Herod, and what do we find? A true prophet appearing? Yes, indeed. Of John the Baptist, Jesus was to say, "A greater prophet, among those born of women, than John the Baptist there is not one" (Luke 7:28). A true priest functioning? Yes! Of Zechariah, the father of John, it is written, "There came to be, in the days of Herod, the king of Judea, a certain priest named Zechariah, of the routine of Abiah, and his wife, of the daughters of Aaron, and her name is Elizabeth. Now they were both just in front of God, going in all the precepts and just statutes of the law blameless" (Luke 1:5,6).

A true prophet and a true priest, but was there a true king? Herod was reported as king of Judea (Matt. 2:3; Luke 1:5), and was the one who had the temple rebuilt, but was he the true king who would grace the temple with his presence? The magi from the east answered that question when they asked, "Where is He Who is brought forth King of the Jews?" This could not be Herod, for Herod was not a king at birth. Indeed, this is a state peculiar to Jesus. Other kings may be born to become king, but they are born princes, and acquire the status of kingship later. Jesus was a King unique in every sense, but He was not immediately recognized as King except by the very few.

Emmanuel

Israel, had they but known it, were in a very privileged position at this time. God, in the person of His Son, was to dwell among them. The name Emmanuel means "God with us" (Matt. 1:23). Jesus introduced God to His people in a new personal relationship, namely, that of Father, and so completely did Jesus reveal God that it could be said that those who saw Him saw the Father (John 14:9). This special relationship implies admission to God's family and implies also companionship and mutual interest and reconciliation, yet Israel soon proved that they were unready to accept their offered privileges. In spite of all the benefits of the kingdom, bestowed upon them in advance - the feeding of the multitudes, the healing of the sick, the raising of the dead - they refused to accept the King, but rather clamoured for Him to be put to death. Could anything seem more tragic?

The prophet of salvation, John, was murdered by another Herod at the instigation of his sister-in-law, Herodias. The just and righteous priest, Zechariah, had died, and the office of chief priest was held by a self-righteous Caiaphas (no descendant of Aaron) who listened to and supported the pleas of those who would betray Jesus (Matt.26:1-16). But what of the King Himself? Acclaimed by the crowd on one day only as He rode into His capital, Jerusalem, He was within a week being led out of the capital to an execution stake. Was God's endeavour to dwell among His people being finally and irrevocably thwarted?

It would surely seem so, and yet, marvel of marvels, that very act which put Jesus on the cross was the means God used to open the floodgates which would lead to the ultimate reconciliation of all in both earth and heaven, as we read in Colossians 1:20, where we find that peace between God and His creation is effected by the blood of Christ's cross.

This is the significance of the rending of the curtain in the temple at the very moment when Christ gave up His spirit to His Father. Note that the curtain was rent from top to bottom, not from bottom to top. This indicates that it was God Who did the rending, not men, just as the passage in Colossians indicates that it was God Who made the peace through the blood of the cross. Men could do nothing to conciliate God, and thus form a basis for reconciliation; indeed, they sought to annihilate the very One and the only One Who could meet this need. Actually Christ fulfilled a

87

dual role; He was both Chief Priest and the Offering which was carried into the most holy place of all - not one made by hands, but heaven itself, there to be offered in the presence of God (Heb.9:23-26). As a result of this, God Himself is truly and finally conciliated to all; for Him to dwell in their midst for ever, it only remains for His creation to become reconciled to Him. However, this will take a long time.

Meanwhile, what else is there to say about the sanctuary which Herod had restored? Though Herod would not know this, it was obviously rebuilt in time to receive the Lord of Glory when He should come to earth as Israel's Messiah, and it is a fact that Jesus on several occasions referred to it as "My Father's house". It was, however, desecrated by the merchants and money changers, whom Jesus twice drove out - once at the beginning of His ministry (John 2:13-17) and again right at the end (Matt.21:10-13; Mark 11:15-17; Luke 19:45,46). The sanctuary was further desecrated by the malpractices of the religious leaders, the scribes and the Pharisees, whom Jesus denounced, as recorded in Matthew 23. Further, and worst of all, the temple failed to recognize the Light within it. The Lord had suddenly returned to His temple, but the temple had rejected the glory of His presence. For all of these reasons, it could not survive, and its utter destruction was duly prophesied by Jesus when He declared judgement upon Jerusalem. He no longer regarded it as "My Father's house", but spoke of it as "your house". "Left is your house to you desolate" (Matt.23:38).

In the first verse of Matthew 24, we read that Jesus went from the sanctuary. The glory of God had departed from the buildings. The disciples endeavoured to impress Him with the splendour of the outward appearance of the edifice, not appreciating that it had become corrupt within, but He countered by asking them, "Are you not observing all these (stones)? Verily, I am saying to you, Under no circumstances may a stone here be left on a stone, which shall not be demolished". It was even then an empty shell; it would become a complete ruin. Its utter destruction by Titus in A.D. 70 fulfilled the prophecy of Jesus to the letter.

The True Temple

In contrast to this, Jesus gave a beautiful picture of another temple - the temple of His body - the temple in which God always delighted to dwell. This, too, would be destroyed, but in three days would be raised up again. The Lord Jesus is the perfect pattern of a true temple. It was never desecrated; no profane utterance ever emerged from it. It was not destroyed for its own sake, but for the sake of others. Because of this, it was raised up again, and elevated to an even higher pinnacle, and now lives for evermore, the temple in which the entire complement of the Deity is dwelling bodily, and in which it delights to dwell (Col.2:9; 1:19).

Chapter Nine

THE BEGGAR AT THE BEAUTIFUL GATE

Before we leave the subject of the temple restored by Herod but condemned to utter destruction by the Lord Jesus, we may perhaps be permitted to refer to one or two events which occurred within its precincts before that destruction took place. There was a period of approximately forty years during which, as a direct result of the Lord's prayer on the cross, the kingdom was again offered to Israel, and during which the prophecy concerning the destruction of the temple was stayed. While the temple thus remained, it was visited on several occasions by the apostles, and a very special incident connected with one of these visits is recorded for us in the third chapter of Acts.

The story of the healing of the lame beggar who sat at the Beautiful Gate of the sanctuary is one of the most touching in the whole of the Scriptures. Here was a man, infirm from birth, piteously pleading for alms, and receiving from the apostles something which had never even occurred to him as a remote possibility.

We all have come across cases which have made our hearts bleed by reason of their apparent utter hopelessness, and by reason, too, of our inability to do more than offer our sympathy as a palliative - people who, like this beggar, have literally to be carried about, and are totally unable to fend for themselves. What joy it would give us if we could put out our hands to some of these and say, "Walk."

Can we possibly imagine the feeling of joy which would surge into this man's mind as he suddenly became aware of the accession of strength to his bones, and found himself, for the first time in his life, able to leap and walk? No wonder that he went into the sanctuary with the disciples and praised God. No wonder, too, that the multitude was filled with awe and amazement at what had occurred.

A Miracle full of Significance

If this event had only a local application, it would surely have been worth recording. If this were an isolated case of a man being cured of a life infirmity, it would gladden our hearts to know of it. But this incident has a far greater significance, and to recognize its meaning, we have to consider both the time and the place of its occurrence.

It is recorded, as we noted earlier, in the third chapter of Acts, and the previous chapter tells of the descent, with power, of the holy spirit upon the twelve apostles gathered in the house of Jerusalem, and of Peter's subsequent proclamation of the Kingdom. Those who welcomed his words were baptized, and in one day about three thousand souls were added to the number of believers. And many miracles and signs came to pass through the apostles in Jerusalem. So the time of this healing of the lame man is during the days when the reoffer of the Kingdom was still open; and the place was the gate (or door) of the sanctuary in Jerusalem, still apparently (though no longer actually) God's dwelling place among the nation of His choice.

In this early part of Acts, we find portrayed in miniature events which will take place when the Kingdom is actually being established; and this incident of the healing of the beggar at the Beautiful Gate is one of a series of happenings which are prominently brought out in these initial chapters. We have, for example, the holding of things in common, and the disposal of acquired property, indicative of the nature of the great jubilee, when purchasers of allotments will return them to their true tenants - to those having the rights to them according to the law. Then we have the healing of this paralytic, the significance of which we will be looking at in a moment. And thirdly we have the summary acts of judgement on Ananias and Sapphira, who fell dead at the word of Peter. In this we have a picture of the swift judgements, which will be visited upon those who rebel against the edicts of the King, Who in that day will be reigning in righteousness, but with an iron club against all wrongdoers.

Undoubtedly, when the Kingdom is set up, acts of healing will be multiplied, and incidents like the one we are considering will indeed be plentiful. As we read in Isaiah 35:5,6, "Then unclosed shall be the eyes of the blind, and the ears of the deaf shall be opened. Then leap as a deer shall the lame, and jubilate shall the tongue of the mute". What a grand time that will be! As humans, there is nothing that awakens our sympathies more than seeing afflictions in others, and nothing that delights us more than to see those afflictions removed. That day will be the greatest day of healing that the world has yet known, and with the healing will come much rejoicing.

But if this episode of the beggar at the Beautiful Gate has many individual counterparts in the coming eon, surely it has for the nation of Israel a collective application as well. In the words of the Concordant Commentary (on Acts 3:2), "Can we not see, in the man lame from his birth, a close likeness to the people of Israel? They had a beautiful way of approach to God, but it availed them little, for they were unable to walk through it into the divine presence. The healing of the lame man was a sign (4:16). As a miracle it was full of significance. To those who read its message it proclaimed the advent of One Who could heal Israel's impotence and bring them, like the lame man, into God's house and fill them with joy and praise. But above all, it was a sign of that day when the desert shall rejoice and blossom as the narcissus, for then shall the lame man leap as a fallow deer. The powers of the eon to come are present in Israel! No wonder the devout and reverent worshippers in the sanctuary are filled with awe and amazement! To them it was no mere prodigy, no unmeaning exhibition of supernatural power, but the key to that Kingdom which was the goal of all their hopes and aspirations.

It meant the end of the Gentile yoke, the sovereignty of Israel over the nations, the coming of Messiah and a thousand blessings for a thousand years."

The Inherent Nature of the Infirmity

Thinking, then, of this national significance, as applied to Israel, let us now examine the incident more closely, and firstly we notice that the man was inherently lame. Such had been his physical constitution all along. That is to say, his affliction came from within, and was not the result of any mishap from outside, such as, for example, might have been caused had he sustained an accident in his youth, or caught a polio germ. On the contrary, we are specifically told that he was lame from his mother's womb. He had never known a time when he was not infirm. Was that true of the nation of Israel? And, if so, wherein lay the cause of its infirmity?

There can be no doubt (as previous studies have indicated) that Israel was completely helpless from birth, and the cause of that helplessness can be seen if we look at Exodus 19, verses 1-6. There we read:

"In the third month of the faring forth of the sons of Israel from the land of Egypt, on this day they enter the wilderness of Sinai.... And Moses goes up to Alueim. And calling to him is Ieue from the mountain, saying, 'Thus shall you say to the house of Jacob and tell the sons of Israel: "You saw what I did to the Egyptians, when bearing you on vulture's wings and bringing you to Myself. And now, if you will verily hearken to My voice and observe My covenant, then you become Mine, special above all the other peoples, for Mine is all the earth. And you become Mine, a kingdom of priests and a holy nation". These are the words which you shall speak to the sons of Israel.'"

Can we now see the origin of Israel's infirmity? This is the passage where God promises to make of them a kingdom of priests and a holy nation, but notice the 'if' clause which precedes God's promise. "If you will verily hearken to My voice and observe My covenant". We know full well that it was quite impossible for Israel to carry out these conditions because of inherent sin, which showed itself in its very worst form in the worship of the golden calf at the very moment when Moses was receiving the new nation's law from God. Truly, as a nation, she was infirm from birth. But now notice the same passage as quoted by Peter (1 Pet.2:9), and note that the 'if' clause is conspicuous by its absence. "Yet you are a chosen race, a 'royal priesthood', a 'holy nation', a procured people, so that you should be recounting the virtues of Him Who calls you out of darkness into His marvellous light, who once were 'not a people', yet now are the people of God, who 'have not enjoyed mercy', yet now are 'being shown mercy.'"

The Stone Rejected by the Builders

No conditions are attached to Peter's statement. Why is the apostle able to detach this passage from the Hebrew Scriptures, and only quote in part? Simply because he has just been telling his readers of a living Stone, rejected by men, yet chosen of God and held in honour, a Stone into which they also "as living stones are being built up a spiritual house, into a holy priesthood, to offer up spiritual sacrifices, most acceptable to God through Jesus Christ" (1 Pet. 2:5).

Mention of the name Jesus Christ brings us back immediately to Acts 3, for it was in the name of Jesus Christ, the Nazarene, that the lame man was commanded to walk. Jesus Christ, the Nazarene. Rejected by men! It was a common saying among the Jews, "Can anything good be out of Nazareth?" (John 1:46). "A Stone, which is rejected by the builders", this is how Peter refers to Jesus in his epistle. Notice particularly that he uses the same simile in Acts 4, verse 11, when he is explaining to the chiefs and elders and scribes of Jerusalem just how this infirm man came to be healed. Let us read from verse 8.

The Beggar at the Beautiful Gate

"Then Peter, being filled with holy spirit, said to
them, 'Chiefs of the people and elders! If we today
are being examined as to the benefaction to the infirm
man, by what he has been saved, let it be known to you
all and to the entire people of Israel, that in the
name of Jesus Christ, the Nazarene, Whom you crucify,
Whom God rouses from among the dead, in this name,
this man stands by before you sound. This is the
Stone that is being scorned by you builders, which is
becoming the head of the corner. And there is no salvation in any other one, for neither is there any
other name, given under heaven among men, in which we
must be saved.'"

Two Significant Numbers

In connection with this story of the lame man, two
numbers are brought to our notice. Whenever numbers
are mentioned in Scripture, they should be carefully
examined, for often they have a special significance.
In this case we have, firstly, the number nine, for
Peter and John went up to the sanctuary at the ninth
hour, the hour of prayer. Did not something else of
very great significance occur at the ninth hour? Was
it not at the ninth hour that the darkness was lifted
from around the cross, signifying that the price of
sin had been paid, and the just demands of God met,
and that the way was now open for blessing to flow,
where before, curses had predominated? It was after
the ninth hour that the beggar at the Beautiful Gate
was healed.

And the other meaningful number in this connection
is the beggar's age, which we find mentioned in Acts
4:22. He was over forty years old. Now, as again we
saw in earlier studies, the number forty is used in
Scripture to denote a period of trial or testing.
Jesus was tested forty days by the Adversary; God allowed Himself to be tested of the Israelites in the
wilderness over a period of forty years (Heb.3:9);
Saul, David and Solomon all reigned forty years to
prove their inability to be the Messiah. This lame

95

man's period of trial was a full forty years; that is to say, his time of testing was complete - perhaps even brimful and overflowing (see Joel 3:13) - and before him lay no more infirmity, but only blessing.

And certainly that will be Israel's experience when the Kingdom is established. As we read again in Isaiah, "The ransomed of Ieue shall return, and they shall enter Zion with jubilation, and rejoicing eonian shall be on their head. Elation and rejoicing shall they overtake, and flee shall affliction and sighing (35:10).

All the prophecies of Isaiah and others relating to the blessings promised for Israel in the Kingdom, indicate that they are primarily for the glory of God. But was the nation thinking very much about the glory of God at the time that Peter and his associates were proclaiming the Kingdom message? Did the beggar, who sat at the door of the temple, ask to be carried inside? No, all he begged for were alms. He had no thoughts beyond the temporal needs of the moment. We must not blame him; in his position, we would probably have done the same. But notice, this man had been taken daily to this entrance to the sanctuary; is it not remarkable that he had never been healed by Jesus, Who surely would have had pity on such a case if it had been brought to His notice? Was it that he and his friends lacked faith in the healing powers of the Lord? It would certainly seem so. The most he expected was a monetary gift; he received instead something far, far in excess. It was not the faith of the infirm man that brought about his cure, but the faith of Peter in the power of the spirit that had been vested in him.

God's Blessings exceed Expectations

It will also be true of Israel in the Kingdom, that they will receive far more than they expect or deserve, for God always gives more and better than men seek, or hope to obtain. It will be equally true of humanity in the eventual outworking of God's purpose.

96

For is not humanity likewise a beggar lying at the very gateway of the temple of God? And is not humanity as a whole infirm from the beginning, for has not death passed through to all mankind as a result of one man's transgression at the beginning? And is not this in order that the grace of God and the gratuity in grace, which is of the One Man, Jesus Christ, may to the many superabound? (Rom.5:12-15).

We are not trying to extend the application of this particular episode in Acts 3; but the One, in Whose name the Israelites will be brought into full possession of the Kingdom, is the same One through Whom all humanity (and, indeed, all creation) will be reconciled to God (Col.1:20). There is, therefore, a limited analogy between the treatment of this lame man by the apostles, on the one hand, and the treatment of humanity by Christ, on the other. Humanity is out of touch with God and shows no great desire to return to His presence, but rather begs from all and sundry for alms. And what are the alms for which mankind is begging? Briefly, they can be summarized in the phrase, "Happiness, peace and prosperity". The glory of God finds little or no place in their thoughts; indeed, even the mention of God, except in a profane way, is becoming more and more absent from their utterances. Their desires are becoming concentrated, to an ever greater degree, on their own immediate well-being, based upon pleas to their fellows rather than to God.

This is particularly noticeable towards the end of the year, when one hears much about what is termed "the Christmas spirit". This is paraded as an example of good will and intentions, and regret is often expressed that such feelings, as are then supposed to be uppermost, cannot pervade the whole year. But how should we analyse this so-called Christmas spirit? For two or three weeks before the festival, the postal mail is increased to an enormous extent, and greeting cards are exchanged between families and friends in all parts of the earth; but the message on these cards is almost invariably for happiness and prosperity at Christmas and in the New year. Nothing there about glory to God; a few cards may convey such a suggestion, but not many.

We think it fair to repeat that mankind has moved so far away from God as to leave Him almost entirely out of consideration, and is looking for happiness, peace and prosperity apart from Him. But the only lasting happiness that men can realize must come through the One Whom God has appointed - the One Whom all the types and shadows of the Hebrew Scriptures portrayed - the One Whom men despise and forget, or to Whom they only pay lip service - Jesus Christ, the Nazarene. He will truly give them far more than they can ever hope for or expect, for their reconciliation to God will mean, not their going into God's sanctuary but God's coming to dwell with them. For in the fifth eon, the day of God, His "tabernacle is with mankind, and He will be tabernacling with them, and they will be His peoples, and God Himself will be with them. And he will be brushing away every tear from their eyes". (What a delightful touch!) "And death will be no more, nor mourning, nor clamour, nor misery; they will be no more, for the former things passed away."

Humanity's reconciliation to God will mean, not just the mere healing of their infirmities, but life itself in its joy and fullness.

God's Ultimate Dwelling Place in Spirit

To return to the episode of the lame man, we know that Israel, as a nation, did not learn anything from this sign, nor yet from the later preaching of the apostles in the sanctuary (Acts 5:17-25). That the offer of the Kingdom was decisively rejected was shown in the murder of Stephen. We remember that the vision granted to Stephen was of the Son of Mankind standing at the right hand of God (Acts 7:56). In Romans 8:34, Christ is described as being "at God's right hand", and in Ephesians 1:20 as being seated" at His right hand". In Stephen's vision, He was seen standing, which indicates that He was ready to come. Also the term "Son of Mankind" connects the vision with Matthew

98

24:30, where the Son of Mankind is described as "coming". Thus, in rejecting Stephen, Israel rejected the Coming One; in stoning Stephen they added his death to their previous murder of God's Son. Not again are the twelve recorded as preaching in the temple; in fact, they are soon reduced to eleven by the murder of James by Herod (Acts 12:2), and their kingdom powers seem to vanish. We read no more of their ministering together. Of course, in the resurrection, when the circle of the twelve is reformed, they will all be functioning again, for they will be seated on twelve thrones, judging the twelve tribes of Israel, as the Master had promised (Matt.19:28; Luke 22:30).

Paul also is recorded as having entered the sanctuary (Acts 21:26), but his presence there caused angry Jews to "throw the entire throng into confusion". By this time, Paul had become anathema to the ritualistic Jews, who, as at all times, urged an obedience to the letter of the law (plus the letter of their subsequently added decrees), and in so doing completely lost the spirit of it. Consequently, they sought all manner of means to bring totally unjust accusations against Paul at every opportunity, and on this occasion they accused him of bringing Greeks into that part of the temple precincts reserved for Jews only, and thus contaminating the sanctuary. "The central wall of the barrier" (Eph.2:14) was still very much of an obstacle for those in flesh, where Israel has the ascendency.

But the time was fast approaching when Paul would reveal that God was about to build Himself a new dwelling place. It is remarkable that both Stephen (in Acts 7:48) and Paul (in Acts 17:24) declare that God is not dwelling in temples made by hands. No, God was in fact already preparing Himself a new dwelling place - "a holy temple in the Lord... God's dwelling place in spirit" (Eph.2:22).

Earthly temples, including even those built under God's directions, might vanish, until there was no stone left upon another, but this dwelling place in spirit would surely endure.

Chapter Ten

TEMPLES OF THE FUTURE

In this series of studies we have covered in some detail the earthly temples that have so far been erected, including the Tabernacle in the Wilderness. The last that we considered was the Temple of Herod, which in A.D.70 was thoroughly destroyed by Titus, who was the son of the Roman Emperor Vespasian, and who nine years later became Emperor himself.

Though still within the Roman Empire, Jerusalem and the temple site lay desolate for many years. In A.D. 326, Constantine reestablished it as a Christian centre, but in A.D.637 it became a Mohammedan city, and remained such (except for a period during the Crusades) until A.D.1917, when the Turkish forces were defeated by the British in the first Great War.

Nevertheless, Islam had established its own Mosque on the temple site, and the Dome of the rock has stood there for many centuries, and still stands.

The Next Temple

What of the future? Undoubtedly, the temple of God must be rebuilt according to the design and measurements outlined in the book of Ezekiel. The prophecy of Malachi, partially realized at the Lord's first advent, must find its complete fulfilment in His second appearance. "Suddenly coming to His Temple, is the Lord Whom you are seeking, and the Messenger of the covenant, in Whom you are delighting. Behold! He comes! says Ieue of hosts" (Mal.3:1, CV).

But it seems certain that there must be a temple built prior to the one prophesied by Ezekiel. We know that the man of lawlessness will be "seated in the temple of God demonstrating that he himself is God" (2 Thess.2:4), and that "the abomination of desolation" will stand in "the holy place" (Dan.9:27; Matt.24:15). We said in an earlier study that once a thing has become desecrated, it cannot be repaired but must be replaced; and if this is true, it would be impossible for the temple, desecrated by the man of lawlessness, to be the one in use for divine service throughout the millennial reign of Christ.

With all the technical advance of the present day, it would not take long for the Jews to rebuild a temple. The chief obstacle would seem to be the Muslim Dome of the Rock firmly fixed on the site. How this difficulty will be overcome remains to be seen. At the moment of writing, Israel occupies the land, and is in possession of all Jerusalem. We are surely approaching the end of the present eon, and wait with interest to see what happens in regard to the forthcoming temple.

The Millennial Priesthood

In the minds of many believers, the millennial reign of Christ is the acme of happiness, peace and prosperity. It never seems to occur to them to ask why, if this is so, it should ever come to an end. Paradoxically, it is the very presence of the temple and the divine service associated with it, that proves that the millennium is not the ultimate in God's relations with mankind. For as long as there is a functioning priesthood (even though the Melchizedek priesthood is superior to the Aaronic), there must be a barrier between God and His people, for the priest is an intermediary between God and those He serves.

During the millennial period, the Lord Jesus will reign as a priest according to the order of Melchizedek. But who was Melchizedek?

He was a most remarkable person. He appears abruptly in Genesis 14:18, where he is described as "King of Salem" and "Priest of the Al Supreme". He brings forth bread and wine and blesses Abram after his return from the smiting of the kings who had captured Sodom (and Lot who was dwelling there). He receives tithes from Abram and then disappears from the record as abruptly as he entered.

Equally abruptly, his name appears in Psalm 110:4. This is most clearly a prophetic psalm, for it looks

101

forward to the setting up of the Messianic Kingdom, and the events which immediately precede it. If ever we require a case to prove the divine inspiration of the Scriptures, this is surely one. How else could David take this isolated incident out of recorded history and give it the application and emphasis required by this prophecy? "The Lord swears, and will not be regretting it, Thou art a priest for the eon according to the order of Melchizedek."

The writer of Hebrews picks up this theme, and repeats it again and again (Heb.5:6,10; 6:20; 7:17,21). He also adds further details concerning Melchizedek. Surprisingly, these tell us nothing about his life, yet reveal him as the type of Christ in His role as King and Priest during the next eon.

Hebrews 7:1-3 reads, "For this Melchizedek, king of Salem, priest of God Most High, who meets with Abraham returning from the combat with the kings and blesses him, to whom Abraham parts a tithe also from all; being first, indeed, translated 'king of righteousness', yet thereupon king of Salem also, which is 'king of Peace'; fatherless, motherless, without a genealogy, having neither a beginning of days nor consummation of life, yet picturing the Son of God, is remaining a priest to a finality."

Fatherless, Motherless, without a Genealogy

It was important that the genealogy of Jesus, as the kingly Messiah of Israel in the days of His flesh, should be well established; in Matthew it is traced back to Abraham, and in Luke back to Adam. (For the full significance of these two genealogies, see notes in the Concordant Commentary about the respective passages of scripture; also the first chapter in this book, pages 10 & 11). It was also essential that the the priests be able to trace and establish their genealogy back to Aaron, (see Numbers 3:10; 16:40 and Ezra 2:61,62, where some were actually debarred from the priesthood because they could not do this). But Christ, as Priest according to the order of

102

of Melchizedek, owes nothing to the flesh. It is the risen Christ Who officiates as Priest in the eon to come, and the only genealogy that will qualify Him for this office is that He is the Son of God (Heb.1:2,8).

In His flesh, Christ could not have been a priest, for he was of the wrong tribe - Aaron was of the tribe of Levi and Jesus was out of Judah - but Melchizedek was not of any tribe; rather, he preceded all the tribes, and took tithes from them all (including Levi) through their father, Abraham, and may be said to have blessed them all through him (see Heb.7:5-10). And so nothing is recorded about the father or mother of Melchizedek. Similarly, nothing is recorded about either his birth or death ("having neither a beginning of days nor consummation of life'), so Christ is to be viewed as the One Who preceded all (Heb.1:10) and Who outlives all (v.11,12). Because of this, He is remaining a priest to a finality. Any question of succession is excluded.

To a Finality

The book of Hebrews reveals that all the ritual and all the sacrifices connected with the Tabernacle and the Temple were but patterns of something far more profound, for they portrayed the sacrifice of Christ Himself, and the final putting away of sin, and His entry once and for all into the holy places as the Chief Priest presenting the sacrifice to God, and finding eonian redemption (Heb.9:12). By this He becomes the Mediator of a new covenant with His people (Israel), in which those who are called may be obtaining the promise of the eonian enjoyment of the allotment (v.15).

There is a sense of finality about the book of Hebrews. The Concordant Version renders the Greek phrase (only used in Hebrews), "eis to diênekes" by the words "to a finality' in each of its four occurrences. The phrase is used to stress that the original sacrifices, requiring to be offered year by year, could never perfect to a finality those approaching.

103

Yet Christ, remaining a priest to a finality, and seated to a finality at the right hand of God, is able by one offering to perfect to a finality those who are hallowed (Heb.7:3; 10:1,12,14).

Then why is the millennial reign of Christ not the concluding eon of God's purpose, as so many believe? It will undoubtedly be a time of happiness, peace and prosperity, but this will only be so because the Lord Jesus Christ, and those associated with Him, will be ruling the nations with an iron club (rod of iron) (Psa.2:9; Rev.2:27; 12:5; 19:15). Christ will be reigning as a priest for the eon according to the order of Melchizedek, who himself was both king and priest.

Christ both King and Priest

Where the offices of Melchizedek are named (Gen. 14:18; Heb.7:1), it is the kingly ones which are mentioned before the priestly. Like him, Christ is first a King and then a Priest. In the Unveiling of Jesus Christ, the throne section comes before the temple section. The promise to Israel itself was that it should be a kingdom of priests (Ex.19:6; 1 Pet.2:9). In each case, the priestly functions are shown to be reliant upon the kingly rule, both being invested in the same authority. This could not have been so with the Aaronic priesthood, for the priests had to be of the tribe of Levi, while the sceptre remained with Judah. But Melchizedek functioned as both king and priest. Genesis states that he was king of Salem, the original name for Jerusalem (Psa.76:2). The inspired writer of Hebrews adds that he was king of righteousness, and interprets Salem as meaning peace.

The book of Hebrews, as its title implies, is primarily for Israel, and is particularly concerned with the blessings that will accrue to that nation in the coming Kingdom, and in showing them how they can enjoy the blessings of that Kingdom to the full. The new covenant, which God through Jeremiah had promised to make with the house of Israel and with the house of

Judah, will come into being (Jer.31:31; Heb.8:13). No longer will it be necessary for them to have annual days of atonement, for Christ's one offering has perfected to a finality those who are sanctified. As a result of this, God will be "propitious to their injustices", and under no circumstances will be "reminded of their sins and their lawlessnesses".(Heb. 8:12). Because of this, they may have "boldness for the entrance of the holy places by the blood of Jesus, by a recently slain and living way which He dedicates for us, through the curtain, that is, His flesh", and "having also a great Priest over the house of God", they may be approaching with a true heart, in the assurance of faith, with hearts sprinkled from a wicked conscience, and a body bathed in clean water" (Heb.10:19-22).

The Concordant Commentary on these verses is instructive. It reads: "The 'recently slain way' is a reference to the path into the temple. On either side were the bodies of the sacrifices which had just been slain, and offered to Jehovah. It, however, was a dead way, and no one but a priest dared enter upon it. The way now lies through the death and resurrection of Christ, hence it is a living way, though recently slain. In the past, even priests dared not venture through the curtain, behind which the Shekinah glory dwelt. Now, however, the Hebrews of every tribe have access, not only into the outer court of the priests, but into the holy place and into the holy of holies, where the high priest went but once a year. He went with fear and trembling, but they are invited to enter with assurance, because of the efficacy of this sprinkled blood and the cleanliness which comes through His word (John 15:3)."

God Dwelling among His People

There are many prophecies in the Hebrew Scriptures which relate to the millennial reign of Christ, and indicate that the God of Israel (Ieue) will then be

dwelling among His people. Among them are the following:

Psalm   Known in Judah is Alueim,
76:1,2   In Israel great is His name.
(CV)   And coming to be in Salem is His covert,
            And His habitation in Zion.

Ezekiel   And the name of the city from that day
48:35(CV), shall come to be, Ieue-is-there.

Zechariah   Thus says Ieue; Return do I to Zion,
8:3(CV)   And I tabernacle in the midst of Jerusalem,
            And called is Jerusalem--the city of truth,
            And the mountain of Ieue of Hosts -
            the holy mountain.

God has chosen Zion for His dwelling place, and He
yearns for it (Psa.132:13,14). From Zion shall go
forth the law, and the word of the Lord (Ieue) from
Jerusalem (Isa.2:3).

We cannot do better than close this particular
study by quoting from some notes in our possession;
they are from the pen of Bro. Alan Reid, and they are
used by permission:

" During the thousand years (the fourth eon), the
Lord Jesus Christ will reign as priest after the
"priest king" Melchizedek order. In association with
their Messiah, His people - the faithful, the resurrected of Israel with the law inscribed on their
hearts - will reign as priests also (Rev.1:6; 20:6).
They will shepherd the nations with an iron club (Rev.
2:27; 12:5; 19:15). Rule, based upon the Temple, will
be in righteousness and will be seen, and acknowledged
to be righteous, but it will be of an order and character which will not tolerate deviation in any form.
The nations will be instructed in the law and in the
ways of God, for from Zion will fare forth His Law.

Isaiah   ' And it comes in the days hereafter,
2:2(CV)   Established shall be the mount of Ieue,
            And the house of the Alueim,

On the summit of the mountains,
And borne by the hills.
And stream to it all the nations. '"

God Tabernacles with Mankind:
The New Earth

The graciousness of Ieue the Alueim of Israel, implicit in His expressed desire to dwell amidst the ancient people of His choice, is a most notable truth, but even so, His people never had unrestricted access to the tabernacle or the temple wherein His glory tabernacled in the past. The divine service associated with His sanctuary permitted none but the high priest to enter within the most holy place, and that only once a year, on the day of propitiation, with the blood of the sin-approach.

Nor during the millennial reign of God's Anointed will the nations enjoy freedom of access to the Temple. Certainly, as we have seen, "all nations will stream" to God's House (Isaiah 2:2), and those of the nations will gather from all lands to worship, for this will be required of them (Zech.14:16-19), but His very glory will be the effective barrier to His august presence.

Tabernacle or temple built by hands and sanctified by the glory of the presence of God, although indicative of divine proximity, can never fully mean the warm closeness of God's companionship, for ritual and priesthood always imply a barrier. But between God and humanity such a warm, vital relationship will yet come to exist, and of this we learn from the testimony of the apostle John in the record we know as "The Scroll of the Unveiling of Jesus Christ":

"And a temple I did not perceive in it [the city, the New Jerusalem], for the Lord God Almighty is its temple, and the Lambkin. And the city has no need of the sun nor of the moon, that they should be appearing in it, for the glory of God illuminates it, and its lamp is the Lambkin" (Rev.21:22,23).

107

This awaits the fifth eon, the new earth, when "the tabernacle of God is with mankind", not just with Israel as hitherto, but with all mankind then on the new earth, "and He will be tabernacling with them, and they will be His peoples, and God Himself will be with them" (Rev.21:3).

The position in the future fifth eon will in a way be reversed, in that, instead of the Shekinah dwelling, condescending to be confined within a Temple, the Lord God Almighty Himself, and the Lambkin, will become the Temple. Humanity will dwell within that blessed Sanctuary, and the all-embracing Presence will in this way tabernacle with mankind.

Chapter Eleven

THE DIVINE SERVICE OF

THE CELESTIALS

In all our studies so far, we have confined our attentions to the various structures made (or to be made) by hands - the tabernacle in the wilderness, the temples of Solomon, Zerubbabel, Herod and those still to come into being either before or during the millennial reign of Christ.

All these were (or will be) erected on earth, and even the holy city, the new Jerusalem, God's future tabernacle with mankind (though possessing no material temple - Rev.21:22) is still located on earth, having descended out of heaven from God.

We have from time to time hinted, without going into the matter very deeply, that God desires a spiritual dwelling-place. He finds this first in Christ, in Whom His Spirit has always dwelt, and in Whom it always found a spirit to respond in kind (John 17:21). He finds it, too, in the ecclesia, which is the body of Christ, for the ecclesia is being "built together for God's dwelling place in spirit" (Eph. 2:22). He will find it ultimately in the hearts of all His creatures, when He becomes All in all. But this takes us to the consummation of His purpose, and there is much intervening, and two eons still to elapse, before this ultimate is achieved.

Before we leave the "temples made by hands", we should look at them again in relation to the divine service of the celestials, which matter is brought to our notice in the book of Hebrews (8:5).

The Importance of Divine Service

Several terms are used in God's Word for "serve" and "service", but in the New Testament, the word latreia (and its associated verbal form, latreuoo) is especially used to indicate divine service, or service

109

for God. (Latreia means "divine service" and latreuoo means "to offer divine service".) Other Greek words are used for ordinary service, such as douleuoo (meaning "to serve as a slave" - see Matthew 6:24, where it is used twice, and Romans 6:6), and diakoneoo (generally used in connection with service for others, such as serving at tables - Luke 10:40; Acts 6:2). The Authorized (King James) Version uses words somewhat indiscriminately, so that it is difficult, without referring to a concordance, to know which Greek word is being used in any particular passage. But the Concordant Version is clear and distinct, and uses the phrase "divine service" wherever latreia and latreuoo occur in the Greek.

Now this theme of divine service is very important. One of God's great judgements against mankind as a whole is that they "offer divine service to the creature rather than to the Creator" (Rom.1:25). This is in total violation of the principle enunciated in the first of ten commandments given by God to Israel through Moses, "Thou shalt have no other gods before Me", and of the truth proclaimed through Isaiah, "I will not give My glory to another" (Ex.20:3; Isa. 42:8).

Among earth's inhabitants, the custodianship of "the divine service" was entrusted to Israel. It was part of that nation's allotment, along with the "sonship and the glory and the covenants and the legislation...and the promises" (Rom.9:4). It had been promised to Abraham, as Stephen reveals in his address (Acts 7:7), for after his seed had been enslaved and illtreated for around 400 years, they were to come out of Egypt, and offer divine service to God in the land which had been promised to them (see verses 4 and 5).

Divine Service - Individual or Corporate

Divine service could be offered either individually or corporately. Individually, it was offered day and night in the temple by Hannah (Luke 2:37) and on various occasions by Paul (Acts 24:14; 27:23; 2 Tim.1:3).

But perhaps the most forceful usage of the term, as applied to individuals, is that of the Lord Jesus, when He applied it to Satan, "The Lord your God shall you be worshipping, and to Him only shall you be offering divine service" (Matt.4:10). What a conversion this will be when the Adversary does indeed offer divine service to His Creator! Yet he is surely included in the second "all" in 1 Corinthians 15:28 ("that God may be All in all"), since the previous verses of this chapter clearly show that only God Himself is excluded from the comprehensiveness of the "all" that is being made subject to Christ.

It is an individual aspect of divine service that is spoken of in Romans 12:1, where it is applied by the apostle to believers in this present day of grace.

In its corporate aspect, it is spoken of by Zechariah in Luke 1:74,75 where he prophesies of Israel being able, at some future time, "to be fearlessly offering divine service to God in benignity and righteousness in His sight all our days", and by Paul in Acts 26:6, where he speaks of "the promise which came by God to our fathers" and "to which our twelve-tribed people, earnestly offering divine service night and day, is expecting to attain". Again, in Revelation 7:9-15, we read of "a vast throng which no one was able to number, out of every nation and out of the tribes and peoples and languages, standing before the throne... of God and are offering divine service to Him day and night in His temple."

The Misuse of Divine Service

Divine service can be offered to false gods, as Stephen (in the address to which we referred earlier) clearly shows in Acts 7:41-43. Such false worship is to be utterly condemned. Again, it can be offered to God, but erroneously, as Jesus prophesied concerning those who would persecute His disciples, and was not Saul of Tarsus one of these (compare John 16:2 with Acts 26:9,10 and 1 Tim.1:13)? Saul, in those days, did not know Christ, yet he had a zeal for God which caused him to persecute the ecclesia, and doubtless he thought that he was serving God thereby. And yet again, divine service can be offered to God, but grudgingly or even feignedly; there are those who are more fond of their own gratification rather than fond of God, but have merely a form of devoutness lacking the power of real devotion (2 Tim.3:5).

How it behooves us to examine our own divine service, and to be certain that we endeavour to give all glory to God thereby. The moment that we begin to entertain the thought of self-virtue in our service for Him, it falls away from the standard which He has set, and may even cease to be divine service. Self-gratification may very easily creep in, and we may soon be priding ourselves with the thought that we are helping God. Yet this is far from the case, for of ourselves we can do nothing. Yet such is the grace of God that even those things that we do of ourselves with the false idea of helping Him, may possibly be blessed by Him.

There is a beautiful example of this in connection with Abraham. We know how, when he was seventy-five years old, he was promised a seed (Gen.12:4), yet ten years passed by and the promise was not implemented (Gen.16:2,3). So Abram, as he then was, took Hagar, Sarai's maid, to wife, and Ishmael was born, and there is no doubt that for thirteen years Ishmael was regarded by Abram as the child of promise. This is made clear in Abraham's plea for Ishmael following the announcement that Sarah herself would bear a son, and his name should be called Isaac (see Gen.17:18). God thereupon indicated that He would establish His covenant with Isaac, yet Ishmael, too, would be blessed, and verse 13 of chapter 21 makes it clear that this blessing is because Ishmael is Abraham's seed. But this blessing of Ishmael, with the consequent multiplicity of Arab races descended from him, would prove an obstacle for Israel (the nation descended from Isaac) for many generations to come, even in fact to the present day. Twelve princes was Ishmael to beget, the equivalent of one for each of the tribes of Israel (Gen.17:20).

The Divine Service of the Celestials

Divine Service in Hebrews

In the book of Hebrews, the phrase "divine service" (either as a noun by itself, or in conjunction with the verb "offer") occurs eight times, and all of these are in connection with the tabernacle and its sacrifices. The first of these is in Hebrews 8:3, and is a most remarkable one, for it introduces a new dimension into our studies when it speaks of "the divine service of the celestials". The full passage reads:

"Now this is the sum of what is being said: Such a Chief Priest have we, Who is seated at the right of the throne of the Majesty in the heavens, a Minister of the holy places and of the true tabernacle, which the Lord pitches, and not man. For every chief priest is constituted to offer both approach presents and sacrifices. Whence it is necessary for this One also to have something which He may offer. Indeed, then, if He were on earth He would not even be a priest, there being those who offer approach presents according to the law who, by an example and shadow, are offering the divine service of the celestials, according as Moses has been apprized when about to be completing the tabernacle. For see, He is averring, that you shall be making all 'in accord with the model shown you in the mountain.'"

It helps us a great deal when we remember that humanity is not the first, nor indeed the greatest, of God's creations. These are to be found in the heavens where there are "sovereignties and authorities and powers and lordships" evidently controlling vast numbers of subjects (compare Eph.1:21 with Col.1:16). That there had been rebellion among the celestials is indicated by the phraseology of Ephesians 6:12, and by the institution of darkness (something foreign to God - 1 John 1:5) before ever man came on the scene (Gen.1:2).

In earlier chapters, and particularly in the booklet "The Place of Humanity in God's Purpose", we have endeavoured to show that humanity was brought into being as a special and separate creation of God,

113

to be used by Him in rectifying the evil wrought by Satan among His prior celestial creation, and in restoring peace between Him and His whole universe. This, we emphasize, is not of men's doing, but of God. Man is the privileged instrument in the divine purpose, not the boastful planner. And though man, down the centuries, has done his best to blunt the instrument, and even to twist the august Hand that wielded it, God has never allowed His hold to be slackened one iota, nor His guiding fingers to be diverted one inch from the path that He has determined beforehand.

So it is from the celestial inhabitants of His universe (as well as from humanity) that God desires to receive worship and divine service; but such worship and such service can only be complete when there is uninterrupted access by the worshipper to the One Who is being worshipped. This has been prevented by the estrangement which has arisen between God and His celestial creatures because of their rebellion, and thus a position has arisen in the heavens which is comparable with that indicated by the tabernacle on earth. In the latter, access to God's presence could only be attained by one man (the chief priest) through his entrance into the Most Holy Place once every year; and the tabernacle on earth is a shadow or picture of a figurative, but true, tabernacle in the heavens, into which Christ, as chief Priest and Minister of the Holy Places, enters with an offering which will perfect to a finality those who are hallowed, and will ultimately restore divine service in its fullness.

Now we can perhaps see why the structure of the tabernacle (and the temple which followed) had to be in full accord with God's directions, for the model shown to Moses in the mountain had to intimate and illustrate (1) the face of Divine unapproachableness and (2) the means by which approach to God was to be restored.

The Dividing Curtain

In the first verse of Hebrews 9, divine service is shown to be a requisite of the "old" covenant which

God made with Israel, and is associated with a "worldly holy place". There follows a brief description of the tabernacle and its contents, including the propitiatory, and it will be noted that stress is placed on the fact that there were two distinct parts, the holy place and the holy of holies; and that, whereas the priests were passing continually into the former to perform the divine service, only the chief might pass into the latter, and that only once a year, and then not apart from blood. We can thus see that, as this model tabernacle was a picture of the true way of approach to God; the erring celestials who wished to offer divine service, would equally be barred from the celestial most holy place, and would of themselves have no means of ever gaining admittance to the presence of God. Thus their divine service would be incomplete; indeed, it would not be so satisfying as was Israel's, for Israel (owing to the creation of a lower stratum of soul-life, namely animals) could obtain a temporary and partial alleviation of their estrangement by the annual entrance of their chief priest, with the blood of the sacrifices, into God's presence, and his exit therefrom with God's blessing for the people he represented.

For the celestials, there was no such annual provision, and not just for the reason that our time features (days, years, etc.) appertain to this earth, and have no part in celestial arrangements. The celestials had no recourse to a lesser creation whose blood could be alleviative. The animals had been given to man (Gen.9:2-4), but humanity was never given to the celestials. Moreover, any thought that the celestials might find a saviour in humanity were dissipated when Satan, one of their hierarchy, caused the very first of humanity to sin, for all offerings must be without blemish. Yet the subsequent offerings made on behalf of Israel on their annual day of atonement (or propitiation) should have indicated to the celestials that a permanent solution of their problem would be provided, and this came to be the case, for Hebrews 9:11 reads:

"Now Christ, coming along a Chief Priest of the impending good things through the greater and more perfect tabernacle not made by hands, that is, not of this creation; not even through the blood of he-goats and calves, but through His own blood, entered once for all time into the holy places, finding eonian redemption."

The blood of bulls and he-goats had only a limited efficacy. It might hallow to the cleanness of the flesh, but it could not make the one offering divine service perfect as to conscience (verses 9 and 13). The blood of Christ on the other hand was efficacious in the cleansing of conscience from dead works, so that the one thus hallowed might be offering divine service to the living and true God (v.14).

The Cleansing of the Tabernacle

With the announcement of the inauguration of a new covenant comes a dissertation on the necessity and value of the blood of the covenant victim, without which the covenant is not ratified and therefore not available. This leads into a remarkable succession of statements in Hebrews 9:18-22, in which it is shown that not only the people (as well as the scroll of the covenant) but also the tabernacle itself and all the vessels of the ministry were sprinkled with blood. Indeed, it is stated that "almost all is being cleansed in blood". This is surely significant.

In Leviticus 16, verses 15-20, we read of the need for the chief priest (Aaron) to sprinkle the blood of the goat of the sin-offering upon and before the propitiatory, to make a propitiation for the holy place, because of the uncleanness of the children of Israel. And this sprinkling of the blood goes on until he has made an end of propitiating the holy place, and the tabernacle of the congregation, and the altar.

Immediately following this propitiation of the holy place, the live goat (scapegoat) is taken by Aaron, and after "the iniquities of the children of Israel, and all their transgressions in all their sins" have

116

been put on the head of the goat, it is sent away by the hand of a fit man into the wilderness. This represents Jesus as the One not knowing sin, Whom God makes to be sin. Just as the scapegoat was sent out into the wilderness, and took away the sins of the people from out of God's sight, so Jesus was sent into the wilderness of God's disfavour, taking with Him the sins of the universe. The darkness, which enshrouded the cross, represents God's turning away of His face from the scene. Note that God did not turn away His face from the cross as such, or from the shame of His Son hanging upon a tree; for, if He had, it would have been dark for the whole of the six hours instead of the last three hours. No, God turned away from His Son when He was the personification of sin itself, and the returning light would be an assurance to Jesus that God regarded the question of sin as having been dealt with to a finality.

The Cleansing of the Heavens

If the contents of the earthly tabernacle required to be cleansed, because of the contamination caused by the uncleanness of the children of Israel, whose representatives were required to touch them, what are we to say about the contents of the celestial tabernacle? These could only be cleansed by the blood of Christ Himself, for He alone of all the sacrifices was of celestial origin, and it is obvious that the blood of animals could not reach so high. He entered not into holy places made by hands, representations of the true, but into heaven itself (v.24).

Here we have an intimation of God's true dwelling place, heaven itself. Many times in scripture He is called the God of heaven. In Psalm 33:14, heaven is described as "His established dwelling" (CV). The context reads:

From the heavens Ieue looks down,
He sees all the sons of humanity,
From His established dwelling
He peers at all dwellers of the earth.

117

celestials also require to be cleansed because of the evil to be found among them. Let it never be forgotten that the arch exponent of all evil, the Adversary of all God's operations, Satan the deceiver, is a celestial himself, and has multitudes of followers. These all require the benefits of the blood of Christ's cross before reconciliation between God and them can be effected. The scripture in Colossians 1:20 covers all in heaven as well as all on earth.

The year by year performances carried out by Israel's priests on the day of propitiation were, or should have been, repeated lessons to the watching celestials - repeated annually to drive them home - but that to which they were pointing could only happen once, or otherwise (it is recorded) Christ "must often be suffering from the disruption of the world" (Heb. 9:26). Why from the disruption of the world? Why not from Adam's transgression? The use of the phrase "from the disruption" clearly identifies the sacrifice of Christ with the needs of the celestials, for the disruption of the world (kosmos) is the moment of scriptural recognition that there had indeed been rebellion among them, coming, as it did, before the creation (and sinning) of humanity.

This one verse (26) of Hebrews 9 takes us, in one sweeping statement, from the disruption of the world to the conclusion of the eons. Though Christ, as a Saviour, is now manifest, sin will not be completely eliminated from the universe until the conclusion of the eons. But the acceptance by God of Christ's offering has made that elimination inevitable. But this wonderful scripture gives further proof that, just as the curtain which veiled God's presence, was rent in the earthly temple at the precise moment of Christ's death, so that spiritual veil which obstructed the approach of the celestials to God, was likewise rent; and there is nothing now, save their own spiritual blindness, to prevent them entering into the presence of God, and offering Him the "logical divine service" which is His due from all His creatures.

Chapter Twelve

"YOU ARE A TEMPLE OF GOD"

In the foregoing chapters in this study, we have
covered (albeit not exhaustively) the various temples
so far erected, as well as the Tabernacle in the
Wilderness, and we have endeavoured to show the connection between this and the divine service of the
celestials. But before we move completely into the
celestial realms, let us take note of another kind of
temple - a temple in flesh.

When we say "a temple in flesh", we do not mean a
fleshly dwelling place of God, but rather a spiritual
dwelling place embodied in flesh. We have this first
mentioned by Jesus Himself. When the Jews demanded to
know by what right He drove the traffickers and the
money changers out of the literal temple, and said to
Him. "What sign are you showing us, seeing that you
are doing these things?" He answered and said to
them, "Raze this temple, and in three days I will
raise it up" (John 2:18,19).

The Jews completely misunderstood His meaning.
Their unenlightened minds were centred and concentrated in the things of the world around them, and of
material benefit in this life, and could not ascend to
take in spiritual matters. They thought only of the
temple of stone, in the precinct of which they stood,
and said, "In forty and six years was this temple
built, and you will be raising it up in three days!"
(John 2:20,21).

Our Lord had in mind His coming demise, and when
later He was roused three days after His crucifixion,
His disciples were reminded of what He had said, and
it was a real stimulus to their faith (v.22).

Our Lord's Words Distorted

On the Jews, the statement of Jesus had an entirely
opposite effect. Later in His ministry, false witnesses came forward to testify against Him by saying,
"He averred, 'I am able to demolish the temple of God

and, during three days, to rebuild it'" (Matt.26:61).
They were false witnesses because they twisted what
Jesus actually had said. Jesus had never suggested
that He would demolish the temple of God, but that, if
they did it, He would raise it again in three days
(John 2:19).

Again, they brought the same blasphemy against Him
as He hung on the cross, and in a more subtle form,
for they incorporated it in a challenge to Him to save
Himself by descending from the cross. In this is
clearly perceived the work of the Adversary, for this
was his final chance (humanly speaking) to thwart the
purpose of God. Of course, we know that he could not
succeed; nevertheless, the test was a real one, intended to take advantage of the Lord's agony of
spirit, and to offer a tempting and easy way out of
His sufferings. "You who are demolishing the temple
and building it in three days, save yourself! If you
are the Son of God, descend from the cross" (Matt.
27:40; Mark 15:29).

If Jesus had tried to save Himself in the way suggested, He would soon have found that He could not
preserve the temple of His body, for His flesh would
have triumphed over His Spirit, and He would indeed
have missed the mark Himself by failing to carry out
the will of God. And certainly He would have been unable to save others, for God's purpose required Him to
settle, through His death, the question of sin once
and for all time. Without this settlement, God's
Spirit could never find a permanent dwelling place
within the hearts of His creatures.

However, such suppositions are purely hypothetical,
since God's purpose was secure from the beginning because of the total and willing obedience of His Son -
an obedience unto death, even the death of the cross.
When Jesus said, as the hour of His agony approached,
"Father, glorify Thy name!" a voice out of heaven
could reply, with full confidence, "I glorify it also,
and shall be glorifying it again!" (John 12:28).

The Jews, who taunted Jesus, would have been horri-
fied at the thought of destroying the temple of God,

though they had been quite prepared to defile it when it suited their gain. But they were quite oblivious of the true temple when the Lord appeared in their midst, and were more than willing to crucify Him, and thus destroy the temple of His body. (The Concordant Commentary on John 2:18 is very informative here.)

Jesus was the One in Whom His Father invariably expressed delight. He was One in Whom God's Spirit continuously dwelt, for He and His Father were one. In that most intimate of conversations which Jesus had with His Father prior to the giving up of Himself in Gethsemane, He showed this oneness by declaring that "Thou, Father, art in Me, and I in Thee" (John 17:21). Even while He was in the likeness of sin's flesh (though not knowing sin), the Spirit of God found its true home in Him.

The Saints are Temples of God

God's Spirit can also find its home in us, for we, too, are declared to be temples of God, even while we are still in flesh. Paul, writing to the Corinthians, declares, "Are you not aware that you are a temple of God and the spirit of God is making its home in you? If anyone is corrupting the temple of God, God will be corrupting him, for the temple of God is holy, which you are" (1 Cor.3:16,17).

This remarkable statement takes on added significance when we realize that it occurs in that same chapter which begins by telling the Corinthians that they were still fleshly, and were walking, not according to God, but according to man (v.4), and that, because of this, Paul could not speak to them as to spiritual, but as to fleshy, as to minors in Christ. It comes after a passage in which Paul reminds them that, though they had all been given a solid foundation on which to build, some will have been building with flimsy materials - the wood, grass and straw of human philosophies and interpretations, all incorporating human endeavour, rather than the gold, silver and precious stones of the divine truths embodied in

the Pauline evangel which declares all to be of God -
and, in consequence, will be in danger of suffering
loss in that day when each one's work will be tested
by fire. But even in this picture, it is made clear
that all concerned will be saved (v.15).

It is easy to see how Jesus, even while in flesh,
could be a habitation of God's Spirit; it is not quite
so easy to see how our bodies, born in sin and shapen
in iniquity, can be; yet, quite clearly, they are, for
Paul says again (in 1 Cor.6:19), "Are you not aware
that your body is a temple of the holy spirit in you,
which you have from God, and you are not your own?!
And yet again (in 2 Cor.6:16-18), "Now what concurrence has a temple of God with idols? For you are the
temple of the living God, according as God said, that
I will be making My home and will be walking in them,
and I will be their God, and they shall be My people.
Wherefore, Come out of their midst and be severed, the
Lord is saying. And touch not the unclean, and I will
admit you, and I will be a Father to you, and you
shall be sons and daughters to Me, says the Lord
Almighty."

The fact is that these bodies are merely "earthen
vessels", covering a treasure within (2 Cor.4:7).
They are "terrestrial tabernacles" in which we are
groaning, longing to be dressed in a more worthy habitation which is out of heaven (2 Cor.5:1,2). They
are "bodies of humiliation", waiting to be trans-
figured, to conform them to the body of Christ's glory
(Phil.3:21). They are "mortal bodies" (Rom.6:12),
waiting to be changed in that day when "this corruptible must put on incorruption, and this mortal put on
immortality" (1 Cor.15:53).

There is a most apt comment in the Concordant
Commentary on verse 19 of 1 Corinthians 6, which perhaps we may be permitted to quote in full. It reads,
"Wherever God dwells is the temple of God, and is hallowed by His presence. It was not the stately buildings or the sacred ritual or even the sacrifices which
hallowed the sanctuary, but the presence of the glory
of God in the holiest of all. The very ground of the

122

desert was holy where Moses met Jehovah (Ex.3:5). So our body, whatever its physical appearance or condition, has become a temple by virtue of the divine Spirit which indwells us. It is no longer ours, but His, and like the tabernacle in the wilderness and the temple in Jerusalem, should allow nothing that defiles to enter its precincts. God does not dwell in temples made with hands, but in the bodies of His saints. Holy conduct and loving acts are the ritual."

To which comment we may perhaps add that it was not Moses, but God, Who chose the spot where they were to meet and the time of the appointment; it was God, and not man, Who designed both the tabernacle and the temple; and it was God, and not we, Who chose us to be His temples. But we noticed, in the comment, the phrase, "the presence of the glory of God in the holiest of all". This brings us immediately to another point.

Two Different Words

Two different words are used in the Greek to describe the temple. First there is the word **hieron** which is translated "temple" 71 times in the King James Version, but is invariably rendered **sanctuary** in the Concordant Version. This word is used to portray the temple building itself, together with all the surrounding area into which the people, as well as the priests, might enter. Its first occurrence is in Matthew 4:5, where we read that the Adversary took Jesus "into the holy city and stood Him on the wing of the sanctuary". Other clear examples of its usage occur in Acts 3, where the word appears no less than six times between verses 1 and 10 in describing the incident of the healing of the lame man at the Beautiful Gate.

Second there is the word **naos** also translated **temple** in the King James Version 45 times, and once translated **shrine** (Acts 19:24). but consistently rendered **temple** in the CV. This refers to the sacred edifice near the centre of the sanctuary, the holy

123

places, and, in particular, the most holy of all, where the presence of God was to be found.

It is instructive to note that the former word, hieron (sanctuary), does not occur after the book of Acts, except once in 1 Corinthians 9:13, "Are you not aware that the workers at the sacred things are eating of the things of the sanctuary? Those settling beside the altar have their portion with the altar". Apart from this one instance, all references to the temple by Paul, and all by John in the book of the Revelation are to the inner sanctuary, and this adds greatly to their significance.

The distinction between the two words is also shown in passages we quoted earlier. In John 2:14, Jesus found those selling oxen and sheep and doves in the sanctuary (hieron), and cast them out of the same, but in verse 19 He said, "Raze this temple (naos) and in three days I will raise it up."

So the temples of our bodies are the figurative equivalent of the inner sanctuaries of the tabernacle and of the temple - the places made holy by the presence of God. We cannot emphasize too often that it is God Who sanctifies us, even as it is He Who chooses us and Who calls us to His service. He sanctifies us by His Spirit.

The Homing of God's Spirit

This sanctification of our bodies by the Spirit of God was dealt with many years ago in an article in "Unsearchable Riches" by Brother A. E. Knoch ("Spiritual Blessings", Vol. XVIII, p.263). With permission, we cannot do better than requote the paragraphs under the heading, "The Homing of the Holy Spirit" (XVIII, p.272).

"Up to the end of Acts the spirit is found on the saints; from Romans through Paul's epistles, God's holy Spirit makes its home in the members of the body of Christ.... The figure of the temple is transferred to our bodies by the apostle, 'Are you not aware that you are a temple of God and the Spirit of God is mak-

ing its home in you?' As the presence of Ieue sanctified the temple, so we are holy because we are His
home. This is the true basis and power of holiness.
It is not in ourselves, but in Him Who homes in us.

"The homing of God's holy Spirit is set forth most
fully in Romans 8:9,11. There we read, 'Yet you are
not in flesh, but in spirit, if so be that God's
spirit is making its home in you.... Now if the spirit
of Him Who rouses Jesus from among the dead is making
its home in you, He Who rouses Christ Jesus from among
the dead will also be vivifying your mortal bodies because of His spirit making its home in you'. This is
the marvellous continual miracle of God's holy Spirit
in this administration; it gives life to the dead. We
should be in constant enjoyment of this resurrection
power, which makes the body of sin, though dead, the
instrument of righteousness.

"The spirit, homing within us, not only hallows our
mortal frame and gives it life, but also guards that
which He has committed to us. Paul charged Timothy,
'The ideal thing committed to you guard through the
holy spirit which is making its home in us' (2 Tim.
1:14). These three passages fully set forth the present place of the holy Spirit of God in contrast with
its place in the past. Then its presence was occasional and extraordinary; now it is the normal experience of all saints. Then God dwelt in temples, now
He homes in those whom He has hallowed."

Our Logical Divine Service

These facts should not leave us unmoved. On the
contrary, they should surely fill us with a deep sense
of humility, coupled with a desire to be pleasing to
the God who hallows us. This is beautifully expressed
by Paul in Romans (12:1,2). "I am entreating you,
then, brethren, by the pities of God, to present your
bodies a sacrifice, living, holy, well pleasing to
God, your logical divine service, and not to be con-
figured to this eon, but to be transformed by the re-

newing of your mind, for you to be testing what is the
will of God, good and well pleasing and mature."

These bodies of ours, made holy by God's indwelling
Spirit, should be kept free from prostitution (which
was Paul's complaint against some of the Corinthians)
and from the worship of idols. Both physically and
spiritually they should be kept apart for the service
of God. We are bought with a price. By all means we
should be glorifying God in our bodies (1 Cor.6:
18-20).

Paul's entreaties as to our conduct are continued
in 2 Corinthians 6:14-7:1, where we read, "Do not
become diversely yoked with unbelievers. For what
partnership have righteousness and lawlessness? Or
what communion has light with darkness? Now what
agreement has Christ with Belial? Or what part a be-
liever with an unbeliever? Now what concurrence has a
temple of God with idols? For you are the temple of
the living God, according as God said, that I will be
making My home and will be walking in them, and I will
be their God, and they shall be My people. Wherefore,
Come out of their midst and be severed, the Lord is
saying. And touch not the unclean, and I will admit
you, and I will be a Father to you, and you shall be
sons and daughters to Me, says the Lord Almighty. Having then, these promises, beloved, we should be
cleansing ourselves from every pollution of flesh and
spirit, completing holiness in the fear of God."

Sonship

The homing of God's Spirit within us brings us into
a wonderful relationship with our heavenly Father. We
find this stated quite plainly in Romans 8. We pick
up again at verse 11, and read through to verse 14.

"Now if the spirit of Him Who rouses Jesus from
among the dead is making its home in you, He Who
rouses Christ Jesus from among the dead will also be
vivifying your mortal bodies because of His spirit
making its home in you. Consequently, then, brethren,
debtors are we, not to the flesh, to be living in

126

accord with flesh, for if you are living in accord with flesh, you are about to be dying. Yet if, in spirit, you are putting the practices of the body to death, you will be living. For whoever are being led by God's spirit, these are sons of God."

This is in line with what the apostle says in Galatians 4:6, "Now, seeing that you are sons, God delegates the spirit of His Son into our hearts, crying 'Abba, Father!' So that you are no longer a slave, but a son". The passage in Romans continues, "For you did not get slavery's spirit to fear again, but you got the spirit of sonship, in which we are crying, 'Abba, Father!'" (Rom.8:15).

So we have not only the Spirit of God dwelling within us, but the Spirit of Christ as well. This is an added bonus. What kind of spirit is this? It is a spirit of obedient sonship, described even more fully in Philippians 2:5-8. "For let this disposition be in you, which is in Christ Jesus also, Who, being inherently in the form of God, deems it not pillaging to be equal with God, nevertheless empties Himself, taking the form of a slave, coming to be in the likeness of humanity, and, being found in fashion as a human, He humbles Himself, becoming obedient unto death, even the death of the cross."

Abba, Father

"Abba, Father" was the expression used by Jesus in the garden of Gethsemane, just prior to His crucifixion, when He said, "Abba, Father, all is possible to Thee. Have this cup carried aside from Me. But not what I will, but what Thou" (Mark 14:36).

This was a true expression of obedient sonship. It acknowledged first the supremacy of God. It witnessed His ability to do all, even to carry aside the cup which God had prepared for Jesus to drink. It admitted the distastefulness of the trial before, but above all, it acknowledged, and acquiesced in, the paramount necessity for the will of God to prevail.

This should be our attitude in prayer. We may desire certain things in life to be removed from us, but our prayer must always be, not what we will, but what Thou. If we pray thus, we shall always be in line with Christ's Spirit, and will have the support of God's Spirit; even when we are not quite sure what to pray for, the Spirit of God will plead for us with inarticulate groanings (Rom.8:26). When our hearts are too full for words, the Spirit within them can still reach God, for "He Who is searching the hearts is aware what is the disposition of the spirit, for in accord with God is it pleading for the saints" (v.27).

It must be, seeing that it is God's own Spirit dwelling within.

The Walk of the Saints

We close this particular section of our study with a few more words from the notes of Brother Alan Reid.

"The consciousness that we are - each individually - the temple, the dwelling place, the home of holy spirit, should provide to each one of us the most powerful and enduring incentive to a walk that is:
worthy of the calling with which we were called (Eph.4:1),
   the evangel of Christ through which we were called (Phil.1:27),
   the Lord into Whom we have been called (Col.1:10), and of
   our God, Who, in His grace, called us into His own Kingdom and glory (1 Thess.2:12).

"Walk in spirit (Gal.5:16) in recognition of the truth that we are temples of God's Spirit."

Dwell in my heart, O God,
  Let it Thy temple be,
That songs of praise may ever rise
  Out of its depths to Thee.

Live in my life, O God;
  Thy Spirit grow in me,
That every day and every hour
  May be in tune with Thee.

Chapter Thirteen

A DWELLING PLACE IN SPIRIT

The saints of today are indeed temples of God, in which His spirit and that of Christ both dwell. This is an individual status; each one of us is such a temple, and we should be aware of that fact, to the extent that it should have a constant bearing on our lives. This was the theme of our last study.

But there is also another aspect of the matter. Individually, we are each a member of that ecclesia which is the body of Christ, and each of us has his (or her) own function within that body (1 Cor.12: 12-31), yet collectively we all form that one body, the complement by which He is completing the all in all (Eph.1:23). Are we then collectively a temple of God? Is it true to say that His spirit dwells within the ecclesia as a whole? To be sure it is. The supporting scripture is to be found in Ephesians 2, verses 19-22.

"Consequently, then, no longer are you guests and sojourners, but are fellow-citizens of the saints and belong to God's family, being built on the foundation of the apostles and prophets, the capstone of the corner being Christ Jesus Himself, in Whom the entire building, being connected together, is growing into a holy temple in the Lord: in Whom you, also are being built together for God's dwelling place, in spirit."

To get the full meaning of this, let us go back to the first chapter of this epistle, and note particularly when we were chosen for this honour. Beginning at verse 3, we read,

"Blessed be the God and Father of our Lord Jesus Christ, Who blesses us with every spiritual blessing among the celestials, in Christ, according as He chooses us in Him before the disruption of the world, we to be holy and flawless in His sight, in love designating us beforehand for the place of a son for Him through Christ Jesus; in accord with the delight of His will, for the laud of the glory of His grace, which graces us in the Beloved."

The Choosing of the Ecclesia

There are only two passages of scripture which describe the choosing of the ecclesia, yet the contrast between them could hardly be greater.

The one in 1 Corinthians 1, verses 26-31 describes our individual calling, and is certainly not flattering to us as human beings. For we are called from among the stupid, the weak, the ignoble, the contemptible and that which is not - five terms in descending order of worldly value - in order that no flesh at all should be boasting in God's sight. We are left so completely denuded of personal worth that we need something from outside of ourselves to make us fit for the calling with which God calls us. God Himself finds the answer to our deficiencies, for He makes us to be in Christ Jesus "Who became to us wisdom from God, besides righteousness and holiness and deliverance". By doing this He takes away from us all right to vaunt ourselves, but gives us the right, if we must be boasting, to boast in the Lord. Paul himself exercised this right in Romans 15:17, when he said, "I have, then, a boast in Christ Jesus, in that which is toward God. For I am not daring to speak any of what Christ does not effect through me."

The other scripture describing our choosing is the one under notice in Ephesians 1:4. "According as He [God] chooses us in Him [Christ] before the disruption of the world."

He chooses us in Christ. No word here about our merits or demerits. But can we think of anything in Christ as being "stupid, weak, ignoble, contemptible or what is not"? The very suggestion could itself be described by any, or all, of those five terms. That which is chosen in Christ is immensely precious in God's sight, because of the love which He bears to the Son of His love. And it is in love, so we read, that He designates us beforehand for the place of a son for Him. From the very first the ecclesia is seen by God to be holy and flawless, and is very precious to Him, firstly because it is the complement of Christ, through which He is to complete the all in all, and secondly because it is in the ecclesia, and in Christ Jesus, that He is to obtain glory throughout all the generations of the eon of the eons! Amen! (Eph.3:21).

Before the Disruption

The ecclesia was chosen in Christ before the disruption of the world. The disruption is that event which is referred to in Genesis 1:2, where we read that "the earth became a chaos and vacant, and darkness was on the face of the submerged chaos". This was before man was created; hence we were chosen in Christ before any of our acts, or indeed the acts of any of humanity (including Adam himself) could have any bearing on the matter, and certainly long before anybody could be classified according to flesh as "stupid, weak, ignoble, contemptible or that which is not". We were chosen on the same principle as Jacob was chosen, for "not as yet being born, nor putting into practice anything good or bad, **that the purpose of God may be remaining as a choice**, not out of acts, but of **Him Who is calling**" (Rom.9:11). The One Who calls is the One Who has first made the choice, and nothing that happens as a result of the disruption can in any way affect the original choice or the calling that ensues.

The God Who chooses us is the God Who chose Israel to be His people, and of that choice it is written, in Romans 11:25-32, "For I am not willing for you to be ignorant of this secret, brethren, lest you may be passing for prudent among yourselves, that callousness, in part, on Israel has come, until the complement of the nations may be entering. And thus all Israel shall be saved, according as it is written,

Arriving out of Zion shall be the Rescuer.
He will be turning away irreverence from Jacob.
And this is My covenant among them
Whenever I should be eliminating their sins.

131

"As to the evangel, indeed, they are enemies because of you, yet, as to choice, they are beloved because of the fathers.

"For unregretted are the graces and the calling of God. For even as you once were stubborn toward God, yet now were shown mercy at their stubbornness, thus these also are now stubborn to this mercy of yours, that they also may be shown mercy. For God locks up all together in stubbornness, that He should be merciful to all."

"Unregretted are the graces and the calling of God". If salvation is assured to all Israel, in spite of all that nation's stubbornness toward God, then it is certainly assured to all members of that ecclesia which is chosen in the Son of His love.

But the fact that they were chosen before the disruption of the world has an added force. Seven matters are described in Scripture as being from the disruption of the world; only three are described as being in existence before the disruption. They are (1) the love which God had for His Son (John 17:24), (2) God's foreknowledge of Christ's sacrifice (1 Pet. 1:20), and (3) the choosing of the ecclesia. These three indicate the motive behind God's purpose, the means by which it is carried out, and the medium through which its end is attained.

God's purpose is centred around the Son of His love. Christ is God's Executive, carrying out that purpose for His Father. Since all is for Christ (Col. 1:17), it is clear that the motive behind God's purpose was the love He bears for His Son, and, through Him, the love He bears for all creation. Clearly His purpose was conceived before the disruption, and since He knows the end from the beginning, the disruption must have been an element in His purpose.

Hence the foreknowledge of the Lambkin, slain from the disruption of the world (Rev.13:8) but foreknown before it (1 Pet.1:20).

And hence, too, the choosing the ecclesia before the disruption, that it might be holy and flawless, completely free from any contamination or other de-

132

fects brought about as a result of the disruption. The ecclesia was chosen in Christ before any suggestion of an Adversary became apparent to creation. Because of its unique position - antecedent to rebellion in its choice in Christ, yet suffering the effects of rebellion because of its choice out of humanity - the ecclesia is especially well endowed to fulfil God's role for it in the display of His grace to all creation. So clearly established in God's mind was this role of the ecclesia that the gift of grace was given to it, in Christ, even before eonian times (2 Tim. 1:9).

Whether we regard the choice of the ecclesia as being made in Christ before the disruption of the world, or whether we regard it, in its individual aspect, as being chosen in the main from the lower strata of mankind, the choice is of God. The two pictures are not contradictory, but complementary to each other. The one in Ephesians is how God sees the ecclesia - holy and flawless in Christ; the one in Corinthians is how humanity would value its members, seeing them only through eyes of flesh, and being unaware of the calling to which they are called. God's wisdom is as different from man's wisdom as is the picture in Ephesians from that presented to us in Corinthians.

Israel's Pre-eminence in Flesh

The choosing of the individual members of the ecclesia from the ranks of humanity brought with it, however, a different problem, which had to be resolved. In the flesh, all privileges were the property of the nation of Israel. Paul, in Romans, asks, "What, then, is the prerogative of the Jew?" and he replies, "Much in every manner. For first, indeed ... they were entrusted with the oracles of God" (Rom. 3:1,2). Later in the epistle he tells us that theirs "is the sonship and the glory and the covenants and the legislation and the divine service and the promises; whose are the fathers, and out of whom is the

Christ according to flesh, Who is over all, God be blessed for the eons! Amen!" (Rom.9:4,5).

The Gentile nations, on the other hand, enjoyed no such favours. Their position is aptly described by Paul in Ephesians 2:11,12. "Wherefore, remember that once you, the nations, in flesh - who are termed 'Uncircumcision' by those termed 'Circumcision', in flesh, made by hands - that you were, in that era, apart from Christ, being alienated from the citizenship of Israel, and guests of the promise covenants, having no expectation, and without God in the world."

The Greek word translated "without God" is the plural **atheoi** (un-placers). Those referred to here were the true "atheists" of Scripture, in that they had no access to Israel's sanctuary (beyond the court of the Gentiles; cf Concordant Commentary, p.290).

Yes, Israel was the nation of God's choice, so much so that He declared, "But you do I know of all the families of the ground (Amos 3:2). Yet the vast majority, though not all, of the members of the present ecclesia are from the nations outside Israel. How could they be the chosen of God?

Paul answers this question for us in 2 Corinthians 5, verses 14-17. Before we quote this passage from the Concordant Version, let us quote verses 15 and 16 from the King James Version - we have a special reason for doing this. There we read, "... and that He died for all, that they which live should not henceforth live unto themselves, but unto Him which died for them, and rose again. Wherefore henceforth know we no man after the flesh: yea, though we have known Christ after the flesh, yet now henceforth know we Him so no more". Note the triple use of the word "henceforth". Whenever a word, or an idea, occurs in Scripture three times in quick succession, it is **very important**, like the threefold use of the world "create" in Genesis 1:27 (this shows the importance of humanity as a creation) and the threefold use of the word "work" in Genesis 2:2,3, which shows the completion of God's work at that time, and the effectiveness of His stopping.

Henceforth

The word "henceforth" occurs nineteen times in the King James Version of the New Testament and is used to translate several Greek expressions, which are variously rendered in the Concordant Version. Each of these occurrences indicates a point of demarcation, that is, a point at which circumstances or conditions change. We are all used to such points of demarcation; we have several in our own lives. At a certain age we become liable to go to school; at a later date, we are considered to be adult and are allowed to vote in elections; later still we may reach a time when we are entitled to a pension. At each of these points, we could insert the word "henceforth", meaning "from now on."

Many of the scriptural usages of this word (or its CV equivalent) are very familiar, for example, those in Matthew 23:39; 26:29; John 1:51; 13:19; 14:7; Rev. 14:13. Acts 18:6 indicates a vital turning point in Paul's ministry. "From now on [henceforth] I shall go to the nations."

There are other instances besides these. All are important, but surely especially so when we find three within the space of two verses, though again we mention that the three Greek expressions are slightly varied, which explains why the Concordant Version renders them differently. The CV is quite correct in doing so, and indeed could hardly do otherwise and remain true to its principles, but in this particular case the King James Version does bring out the point that there is a threefold demarcation here.

Let us now quote the passage in full from the Concordant Version, but insert [in brackets] the word "henceforth" where it occurs in the King James Version, so that the three lines can easily be picked out.

Beginning then at verse 14, we read, "For the love of Christ is constraining us, judging this, that if One died for the sake of all, consequently all died. And He died for the sake of all that those who are

living should by no means still [henceforth] be living
to themselves, but to the One dying and being roused
for their sakes. So that we, from now on [henceforth]
are acquainted with no one according to flesh. Yet
even if we have known Christ according to flesh,
nevertheless now [henceforth] we know Him so no
longer. So that, if anyone is in Christ, there is a
new creation: the primitive passed by. Lo! there has
come new!"

In this passage, the three points covered by the
demarcation are:

1. Those who can count themselves as living, no
   longer live to themselves, but to Christ.
2. We are acquainted with no one according to
   flesh.
3. No longer do we know Christ according to flesh.

The Discarding of the Flesh

It is clear from a reading of the whole passage
that we have come to a crisis point in Paul's teach-
ings. This crisis is one where the flesh is completely discarded by those who are in Christ. Paul
has been gradually building up his thought to this
position through his two Corinthian letters. These
letters are the earliest writings of Paul (apart from
his two epistles to the Thessalonians, in which there
is no mention of the flesh and therefore no conflict
between flesh and spirit). The conflict begins in
first Corinthians, and is discerned against a background of division and discord, in the preaching of
the cross. For on the cross the flesh (in the person
of the incarnate Son of God) was crucified. Indeed,
we may well say that, in the crucifixion of Christ,
the flesh fulfilled the main purpose for which it was
created in order to provide a form in which God's Son
could appear and give His life for the universe - the
flesh, in fact, being a form of creation subject to
death (cf Heb.2:6-9).

Let us then briefly note how, in these two letters
to the Corinthians, there is a steady and progressive

disparagement of the flesh until it is discarded altogether in the passage we are considering. We quote a few successive scriptures to establish this trend.

"Not many wise according to the flesh...God chooses (1 Cor.1:26).

"So that no flesh at all should be boasting in God's sight" (1 Cor.1:29).

"The soulish man is not receiving those things which are of the spirit of God, for they are stupidity to him" (1 Cor.2:14).

"And I, brethren, could not speak to you as to spiritual, but as to fleshy, as to minors in Christ. Milk I give you to drink, not solid food, for not as yet were you able... you are still fleshly. For where there is jealousy and strife among you, are you not fleshly and walking according to man?" (1 Cor.3:1-4).

Chapters 5 to 11 continue to deal with matters pertaining to the flesh, in conformity with Paul's statement that he could not speak to the Corinthians as spiritual, but must continue to regard them as fleshy, and address them accordingly. Only in chapter 12 does he begin to speak of spiritual endowments.

But in chapter 15 we come across a very significant passage, beginning at verse 45, "If there is a soulish body, there is a spiritual also. Thus it is written also, The first man, Adam, 'became a living soul'; the last Adam a vivifying Spirit. But not first the spiritual, but the soulish, thereupon the spiritual. The first man was out of the earth, soilish; the second Man is the Lord out of heaven. Such as the soilish one is, such are those also who are soilish, and such as the Celestial One, such are those also who are celestials. And according as we wear the image of the soilish, we should be wearing the image also of the Celestial."

Here we have the first intimation of a new humanity (to be described in more detail in later epistles). As the old humanity, begun in Adam, was soulish, so the new humanity, begun in the last Adam (Christ) is spiritual. And the two will not mix, for in verse 50 Paul avers that "flesh and blood is not able to enjoy an allotment in the kingdom of God". Thus the way is being paved for the final discarding of the flesh in 2 Corinthians 5.

This is done in a series of quick statements. First, the apostle establishes that One died for the sake of **all** (v.14). The use of the word "One" emphasizes the unique standing of Christ as the "One not knowing sin" (v.21) in contrast to the "all", who have missed the mark.

Next, Paul deduces that, if One died for the sake of all, then all died. This is a piece of divine logic. Though in men's eyes, the old humanity might continue for many generations, in God's sight it had fulfilled the main object for which it had been created in Adam, and should now be regarded as dead in order that Christ might be the Head of a new humanity, begun in Himself.

From this it follows that "those who are living should by no means still be living to themselves, but to the One dying and being roused for their sakes" (v.15). Living to oneself implies attachment to Adam and the old humanity; this must give way to living to Christ.

The next fact is the logical outcome of all this. It is that we who are Christ's, are acquainted with no one according to flesh (v.16), for there is neither present nor future for anyone in that which God regards as dead. From this, the startling conclusion is drawn that, even if we have known Christ according to flesh (and who is more deserving to be known in this way?), from now on we know Him so no longer. That is to say, we are no longer to look upon Him as the incarnate One (in which case He would still be a Jew, ministering primarily to Israel), but rather to see Him in His present glorified existence as the risen and ascended Lord, a vivifying Spirit, rejoicing in the full power of resurrection might and God-given authority, Who will fill us with His spirit, so that we, too, may be rejoicing in newness of life.

The New Creation

Now we are ready for the complete break with the flesh. "So that, if anyone is in Christ, there is a new creation: the primitive passed by. Lo! there has come new!"

The former humanity is now seen to have been a primitive phase - a temporary tabernacle existence created only to be demolished when the time came for it to make way for a new humanity, created in Christ. That time has now come, though it is apparent only to those of faith, who see the old humanity as having been destroyed at the cross. Though it may seem to continue to exist, it is scripturally regarded as dead (cf Rev.20:12). It has no power within itself to please God. "For" says Paul, "I am aware that good is not making its home in me (that is, in my flesh)", and again, "The disposition of the flesh is death" and "Those who are in the flesh are not able to please God" (Rom.7:18; 8:6,8).

The new creation, of which the new humanity in Christ is a part, is not a development of the old. It would not be a creation if it were. The new heavens and new earth of Isaiah 65:17 do not bring forward anything of the old; on the contrary, it is stated that "the former shall not be remembered, nor come upon the heart". Again, in Revelation 21:4, "The former things passed away". In 2 Corinthians 5:17 it is, "the primitive passed by" (ta archaia, the primitive things).

To Paul, the new creation meant that the world was crucified to him, and he to the world; there was no longer any living connection between them. The privileges of the flesh (as typified by circumcision) meant nothing (cf Gal.6:14,15). Indeed, in Christ all fleshly distinctions vanish; there is no longer Jew or Greek, slave or free man, male or female, for we are all one in Christ Jesus (Gal.3:28).

A Dwelling Place in Spirit

It is in the new creation that the ecclesia is seen as God's dwelling place in spirit, for that which would have confined God's blessings to Israel has been passed by. We shall look into this further.

****

Part Two

We have already shown how Paul established a firm line of demarcation between flesh and spirit, and came to a point in his teaching where he completely discarded the former in favour of the latter. This was in 2 Corinthians 5:14-17. The moment that he declared the fact of a new creation, the former was once and for all passed by.

In this study, we wish to enlarge upon a few of the points last mentioned, and in particular show the wideness of the gulf which exists between flesh and spirit, and which forms the theme of much that occurs in the Roman epistle. Always let us remember that, in spite of the order of the epistles in God's Word, the two letters to the Corinthians, as well as the one to the Galatians, were written before Romans. Thus, when Romans was written, Paul had already passed the line of demarcation represented by the three henceforths (KJV), or their CV equivalents, of 2 Corinthians 5: 14-16. He could write Romans in the knowledge that he had already spoken of a new creation. It is important that we should realize this when studying Romans.

Flesh versus Spirit in Galatians

The same conflict between flesh and spirit occurs in the argument of the Galatians letter. Chapter 5:

16-18 reads, "Now I am saying, Walk in spirit, and you should under no circumstances be consummating the lust of the flesh. For the flesh is lusting against the spirit, yet the spirit against the flesh. Now these are opposing one another, lest you should be doing whatever you may want. Now, if you are led by spirit, you are not still under law."

There follows a comprehensive list of the works of the flesh - adultery, prostitution, uncleanness, wantonness, idolatry, enchantment, enmities, strifes, jealousies, furies, factions, dissensions, sects, envies, murders, drunkenness, revelries, and the like of these - and Paul adds that "those committing such things shall not be enjoying the allotment of the kingdom of God."

Let us not think for a moment that, because some of these things sound so horrible, that we are above them. These are the natural works of the flesh, and if we are delivered from them, it is only because of the abiding Spirit of God within us. And that Spirit can only abide within us because God counts us as being a new creation in Christ, a creation in which the flesh has no part.

In contrast to the works of the flesh, we have a description of the fruit of the spirit - a single fruit (not fruits, but a composite one), made up of nine elements: love, joy, peace, patience, kindness, goodness, faithfulness, meekness, self-control.
Against such things there is no law, for law operates against the flesh, not against God's Spirit. Then Paul adds, "Now those of Christ Jesus crucify the flesh together with its passions and lusts."

The conflict between flesh and spirit is carried forward into the next chapter. In verses 7 and 8 we read, "Be not deceived, God is not to be sneered at, for whatsoever a man may be sowing, this shall he be reaping also, for he who is sowing for his own flesh, from the flesh shall be reaping corruption, yet he who is sowing for the spirit shall be reaping life eonian". And the whole matter is summed up in verses 11-16. The subject is so important that Paul writes

141

in large letters in his own hand, so that there shall be no mistake, and, as we quote further, let us note that in verses 14 and 15, we have reached the same conclusion as in 2 Corinthians 5:14-17, namely, a new creation.

"Whoever are wanting to put on a fair face in the flesh, these are compelling you to circumcise only that they may not be persecuted for the cross of Christ Jesus. For not even they who are circumcising are maintaining law, but they want you to be circumcised that they should be boasting in that flesh of yours. Now may it not be mine to be boasting, except in the cross of our Lord Jesus Christ, through which the world has been crucified to me, and I to the world. For in Christ Jesus neither circumcision nor uncircumcision is anything, but a new creation. And whoever shall observe the elements by this rule, peace be on them, and mercy, and on the Israel of God."

The Flesh condemned in Romans

The line of demarcation between flesh and spirit is expressed (as we have seen) in both the Corinthian letter and the Galatian one by the term "a new creation". In Romans, it is expressed by the term, "being justified", and the break occurs, with great abruptness, in chapter 3, verse 24. Notice the two phrases which come next to each other at this point, "For all sinned and are wanting of the glory of God" and "Being justified gratuitously in His grace, through the deliverance which is in Christ Jesus". Justification paves the way for conciliation, and peace; this is a favour which is agreeable to the thought of the new creation, where the old, with all its enmity, is passed by.

From Romans 1:18 to 3:20, Paul deals with the malpractices and inherent evils of the flesh, and leaves it defenseless (2:1). Although the Roman epistle is concerned with an evangel which has, as its basis, the righteousness of God, this particular portion commences with the revelation of His indignation against a fleshly humanity, which deserves nothing better, seeing that, though men have a knowledge of God, not as God do they glorify Him or thank Him (1:21). Because of this, God ceases any longer to enlighten them, but allows their unintelligent heart to become darkened. Three times in the ensuing verses God "gives them over" to the evil propensities of the flesh (the lusts of their hearts, dishonourable passions, a disqualified mind - 1:24,26,28), and the result is depravity and wickedness consequent upon their allowing full rein to the desires of the flesh - the uncontrolled soulishness of their carnal selves.

The second chapter truly shows man to be without defense; in whatever way he judges another he invariably judges himself, and he is continuously hoarding up for himself indignation in that day when the just judgements of God will be revealed, when He will be paying each according to his acts. With God there is no partiality, and the Jew, in spite of his prerogatives, is not to be privileged, for both Jews and Greeks are seen to be all under sin (Rom.3:9), even as it is written that "not one is just, not even one. Not one is understanding. Not one is seeking out God."

In these words, and those which follow, Paul is condemning the flesh. In verse 19, he continues, "Now we are aware that, whatever the law is saying, it is speaking to those under the law, that every mouth may be barred, and the entire world may become subject to the just verdict of God, because, by works of law, no flesh at all shall be justified in His sight, for through law is the recognition of sin."

At this point we have reached an impasse. There is no way, humanly speaking, by which man can be justified. Without law, the flesh, left to its own devices, turns against God, and fulfils the conditions of Romans 1:26-32. This was evident before the deluge of Noah's day, when there was no law; in that second eon humanity had become so corrupt and violent that God saw fit to destroy them all apart from Noah and his family. The law later given to Israel was a restraining influence, but it could not change the nature of

143

the flesh, and thus could only bring about the recognition of sin. That is to say, the flesh, by works of law, could not become justified in God's sight, because of its own inherent inability (through its soulishness) to keep the law; thus the law only made its sinfulness apparent. Thus, without law or with law, every mouth is barred before God - no excuses can be offered - and the entire world becomes subject to His just verdict.

The Impasse Broken

It is at this precise moment, when all seems to be irretrievably lost, and the prospect utterly hopeless, that the apostle makes a most remarkable declaration, beginning with the arresting connective, "Yet now" (Rom.3:21). (In passing, note how this connective is used in 1 Corinthians 15, verse 20. From verse 12 to verse 19, we have a mounting despair, based on the tentative supposition that Christ is not roused from among the dead - in such a case, our faith is vain, for we are still in our sins; even those who are put to repose in Christ are perished, and we are more forlorn than all men because our every hope is shattered. But what a difference the "Yet now" makes! "Yet now Christ has been roused", and this means that beyond any doubt all who have died in Adam will be made alive - vivified - in Christ, to Whom all will be made subject; that all enemies shall be put under His feet, that death itself will be abolished, and that God will be All in all. From utter abandonment in death to the highest sphere of living, with the glory of the ever indwelling presence of God within each one of us - this is the extent of the impetus given to God's purpose by the "Yet now has Christ been roused". The rousing of Christ makes the consummation inevitable, and this is made clear in these verses.)

If the "Yet now" of 1 Corinthians 15 is God's answer to the problem of death, then the "Yet now" of Romans 3 is His answer to the question of sin. "Yet now, apart from law, a righteousness of God is manifest (being attested by the law and the prophets), yet a righteousness of God through Jesus Christ's faith, for all, and on all who are believing."

This sounds marvellous, as indeed it is - "a righteousness of God for all, and on all who are believing" - yet the next phrase brings us back to reality with a bump. For lest any, who are believers, should think that because of their belief they have some merit which might entitle them to some preference in the matter of justification - some benefit not shared by others - Paul emphasizes that "there is no distinction, for all sinned and are wanting of the glory of God."

How then are any of us to attain to this righteousness, if we cannot contribute anything of ourselves? The answer is declared unequivocally in an expression which incorporates all the majesty, all the wisdom and all the love of God, and which expresses in a phrase all the provision of a caring Creator for His erring creation, which He has never once allowed to slip out of His grasp - "Being justified gratuitously in His grace, through the deliverance which is in Christ Jesus."

Notice here the succession of terms indicative of human helplessness: **Being justified** - requiring to be made right with God; **gratuitously** - without a cause, without anything in oneself that would give God reason for doing this; **in His grace** - purely as a favour; unearned; **through the deliverance** - requiring a rescue act; **which is in Christ Jesus, Whom God purposed** - not in oneself, but in the One Whom God appointed.

By this means of deliverance, ordained and executed by God, all boasting is debarred (v.27). The flesh is excluded.

The Importance of the New Creation

This deliverance is the portal to the new creation, for it is "in Christ Jesus", and "if anyone is in Christ, there is a new creation". With justification, our standing with God is completely changed. We may

be having peace towards Him because of the conciliation He has effected through the death of His Son. He
sees us now as righteous in Christ, and our knowledge
of this should be reflected in our whole attitude to
life. So radical is this change that Paul can declare
that "nothing, consequently, is now condemnation to
those in Christ Jesus. Not according to flesh are
they walking, but according to spirit, for the
spirit's law of life in Christ Jesus frees you from
the law of sin and death" (8:1,2).

The flesh does not lightly relinquish its claim upon
us. On the contrary, it will seek to maintain its
hold until the very moment that we are changed (1 Cor.
15:51). Chapters 6 and 7 of Romans look at the strug-
gle between flesh and spirit and discuss it in some
detail. The spirit sees the flesh as dead. The passage in 2 Corinthians 5:14,15 has a correspondence
with Romans 6:8-11. If we believe that Christ died
for the sake of all, and that consequently all died,
then we should also be reckoning ourselves to be dead
to Sin, yet living to God in Christ Jesus, our Lord.

The highest spiritual observance imposed upon the
flesh was the law of God, which was holy and just and
good. Yet all of those who strove to keep it failed
because of the dominance of sin in the flesh. In the
minds of men, the only alternative to law is anarchy.
Yet anyone, in this era of grace, who still wishes to
be under law, will become conscious of his own inability to attain the ideal, and will experience the
conflict between body and mind as described in Romans
7. In verses 18-20 Paul says, "For I am aware that
good is not making its home in me (that is, in my
flesh), for to will is lying beside me, yet to be
effecting the ideal is not. For it is not the good
that I will that I am doing, but the evil that I am
not willing, this I am putting into practice. Now if
what I am not willing, this I am doing, it is no
longer I who am effecting it, but Sin which is making
its home in me."

The succeeding verses show that, in such a conflict, the flesh will always come out on top; the war

in our members, warring against the law of our minds, will lead us into captivity to the law of sin which is in our members. One thing alone saves us from such wretchedness as this condition implies, and that is grace. For this rescuing agent, Paul thanks God through Jesus Christ, our Lord, and so, too, should we. It is God Who supplies this grace, which operates to secure our initial justification ("Being justified gratuitously in His grace") and attends us in every stage of our journey through life. Because of His grace, we can, indeed, be counting ourselves as dead to sin, yet living to God in Christ Jesus, our Lord.

Nothing Condemns, Nothing Separates

In the eighth chapter of Romans, we have a series of arguments gathering momentum as the subject progresses. The chapter opens with the word "Nothing" (in the absolute - not one thing) "is now condemnation to those in Christ Jesus" and closes with a tenfold nothing (equally absolute) - "neither death nor life, nor messengers, nor sovereignties, nor the present, nor what is impending, nor powers, nor height, nor depth, nor any other creation, will be able to separate us from the love of God in Christ Jesus, our Lord."

In between, we have the clarification of our position and status as participants of a new creation in Christ. We are not walking according to flesh, but according to spirit, for the spirit's law of life in Christ Jesus frees us from the law of sin and death. God, by sending His own Son in the likeness of sin's flesh and concerning sin, has condemned sin in the flesh that the just requirement of the law may be fulfilled in us. Nothing that the law might require is beyond fulfilment by those who walk in spirit. Though they are not bound by the law to obey its letter, as were Israel in the flesh, grace leads them to act far beyond its spirit.

In the next few verses, the gap between flesh and spirit is shown to be wide and, indeed, unbridgeable.

Those who are in accord with flesh are disposed to that which is of the flesh, yet those who are in accord with spirit are disposed to that which is of the spirit.. The disposition of the flesh is death; that of the spirit is life and peace. The disposition of the flesh is enmity to God; it is not subject to God's law, for (as we saw earlier) it is not able because of its own soulish nature. (It was this inherent soulishness which caused man to sin in the first place, and has caused all to sin ever since - it cannot be erased from the flesh). Thus we are led to the absolute statement, "Now those who are in flesh are not able to please God."

This brings us to the points raised in earlier studies in this book. We are not in flesh, but in spirit, if so be that God's Spirit is making its home in us. And if we are being led by God's Spirit, then we are sons of God, and able to cry, "Abba, Father". And, more than that, the spirit itself is adding its witness to our own spirit that we are children of God. "Yet if children, enjoyers also of an allotment, enjoyers, indeed, of an allotment from God, yet joint enjoyers of Christ's allotment, if so be that we are suffering together, that we should be glorified together also." (Rom. 8:17).

This is a far cry from the existence enjoyed by God's people in the flesh. Truly God dwelt with Israel when the tabernacle was in their midst, but He was hidden from their fleshly eyes, and only the chief priest was allowed to enter into His presence on their behalf, and that only once a year, and with blood. But we, living in the spirit of the new creation, where soulish flesh has no place, are granted free and unrestricted access to God, the blood of Christ having opened the way; and God Himself, through His Spirit, dwells within us, both individually and collectively. He has an allotment among the saints (Eph.1:14), in whom He will find glory "throughout all the generations of the eon of the eons" (Eph.3:21).

What we have been endeavouring to do in this particular study is (as mentioned at the beginning) to show the complete gulf that lies between flesh and spirit. It is foolish to try to mix them, or to try to carry over any aspirations or works of the flesh into our spiritual lives. We should be living in the spirit of the new creation, where our former state is regarded as being "passed by", and where we have the assurance that we are, indeed, sons of God, inhabited by His indwelling Spirit.

Chapter Fourteen

THE MINISTRY OF THE ECCLESIA

In our last few studies, we have been showing how Paul differentiates between flesh and spirit, and how the flesh is gradually discarded in favour of the spirit. We have also been trying to show how the ecclesia, which is the body of Christ, is being made the home of God's Spirit - this both individually and collectively.

We are now ready to consider the question of "God's dwelling place in spirit" from the level of the Ephesian epistle - the letter in which this phrase actually occurs.

The Scope of the Ephesian Epistle

The epistle opens with a statement of the writer's credentials - "an apostle [one commissioned and sent forth] of Christ Jesus [the risen Lord Who is ascended to the right hand of God] through the will of God" [through the desire and direction of Him Who is the Supreme Being in the universe]. These credentials give Paul the authority to proclaim the wonderful truths of this epistle. No less authority than this would be adequate to give credence to the revelation contained in its teaching.

Having established his own position in relation to the letter, Paul then clarifies the position of those to whom it is addressed. It is sent "to all the saints who are also believers in Christ Jesus."

Note the words, "who are also believers" and especially note the phrase, "in Christ Jesus". This letter is not for minors; it is for mature saints, who have a firm belief in the Christ of glory (as distinct from a belief in the Jesus of His humiliation on earth). Such believers have a special status in Christ, as we shall see presently. For the moment, let us just say that the truths, which Paul will reveal in this letter, will require much faith on our part if we are to accept them, for he is going to take us away from the confines of earth altogether, and to transport us mentally and spiritually into the celestial regions. This is a sphere in which the flesh cannot possibly have any part, firstly because it is physically tied to the earth, and secondly because it is mentally incapable of discerning the things of the spirit. These can only be revealed to us by God's Spirit (1 Cor.2:10-16), and the most astounding fact is this, that God's Spirit will search the very depths of Himself in order to reveal His truth and His purpose to us. In the Ephesian letter, we are taken not only into the depths, but into the breadths and lengths and heights as well. That is why Paul needed to state his credentials, for what he tells us in this epistle is far beyond the knowledge, perception and inventive power of even the most gifted of men.

The letter plunges us, without any delay, right into the midst of the celestial realms, thus: "Blessed be the God and Father of our Lord Jesus Christ, Who blesses us with every spiritual blessing among the celestials, in Christ, according as He chooses us in Him before the disruption of the world, we to be holy and flawless in His sight, in love designating us beforehand for the place of a son for Him through Christ Jesus; in accord with the delight of His will, for the laud of the glory of His grace, which graces us in the Beloved."

The Heavens in Relation to the Earth

The reference to the disruption of the world immediately connects this epistle with the first two verses of Genesis. There we learn that, "in a beginning" God created the heavens and the earth; but, after this brief statement, little more is said about the heavens. Rather the Scriptures concentrate upon the earth. "The earth became a chaos and vacant...." All through the rest of the Hebrew Scriptures, and the greater part of the Greek Scriptures, too, the earth is the scene of subsequent action, and the heavens are mentioned only as something "above the earth."

151

Now we know that, in reality, the heavens surround the earth, which is a revolving ball in space, hanging, as it were, upon nothing, as Job 26:7 would indicate. The heavens are above the earth only in the sense that they appear from the earth to be above it. Further, if we except the Deity, the inhabitants of the heavens are revealed on occasions, but nearly always in reference to earthly happenings, as when messengers appeared to Abraham to announce the destruction of Sodom and foretell the birth of Isaac, or when a multitude of them were manifest at the birth of Jesus.

Thus, throughout all the Scriptures (apart from the prison epistles of Paul), the earth, as the stage upon which God's purpose is being enacted, is the centre and focus of all the activity, and the heavens are, in the main, above and outside of the action. The occupants of the heavens may be directing the action (as in the case of God and the Lord Jesus, or they may be obstructing (as in the case of Satan); they may be praising God by obeying His will (like Gabriel and Michael), or they may be rebelling against Him (like those who form the "spiritual forces of wickedness among the celestials" of Ephesians 6:12).

In this Ephesian epistle, Paul abruptly, and without warning, transfers the scene of action from the earth to the heavens, and makes no apology for doing so. On the contrary, he infers that our blessings are greatly increased as a result of this, for he declares that God is blessing us "with every spiritual blessing among the celestials". Five times in this letter he is to use the phrase, "among the celestials", en tois epouraniois, which clearly indicates that he is speaking of beings outside of earth's inhabitants. What actually happens is that God is revealing through Paul how He is to deal with affairs that are extraneous to this earth. He reminds us that He has a creation which occupies a realm outside the confines of this planet - a creation which is in view when the word heavens is used in Genesis 1:1 - and (marvel of marvels) He incorporates us, members of the ecclesia

152

which is the body of Christ, within that primeval creation. For we were chosen in Christ before the disruption of the world, and this was at a time when only celestial beings were in existence.

Humanity speculates today as to whether there are other beings in the universe besides those on earth, and tentatively comes to the conclusion that there is probably some other planet (or planets) revolving round some distant sun, with inhabitants possessing some measure of intelligence like ourselves. Its whole conception is, of necessity, vague, because it has no proof, having, in the main, turned its back on the only volume, the Word of God, which could supply an answer to the question.

Well, the Scriptures assert quite plainly that there are inhabitants of the celestial realms, but they are not made of flesh and blood, but are spirit beings of infinitely greater powers of perception than humans. These extra powers, however, have not made them immune from sin and rebellion. As we saw earlier, Ephesians 6:12 tells us that there are "spiritual forces of wickedness among the celestials". Moreover, the letter to the Colossians makes it clear that reconciliation has to be effected with both those on earth and those in the heavens (Col.1:20).

Everything in the book of Ephesians must be considered with the celestials in mind. It is from their numbers that we must find those whose original rebellion against God brought about the disruption. The disruption (with its accompanying darkness) is the scriptural indication that rebellion has taken place, and that is why it is such a line of demarcation in God's Word. Things may date from the disruption, in which case they suffer from the effects of the disruption, or (in three cases) they date from before the disruption, in which case the disruption makes no impression upon them. One of these last is the ecclesia, chosen "in Christ" before the disruption of the world.

The Status of the Ecclesia
as Christ's Complement

The fact that the ecolesia is chosen "in Christ" gives it a status of power and authority in the universe; the fact that it is chosen before the disruption gives it a quality of "holiness and flawlessness" which it will ever preserve. It is a quality which is consistent with its being the complement of Christ, for He, when He came to present Himself at Golgotha, was the "One without sin", an Offering without spot or blemish of any kind. The ecclesia, as the body of Christ, must be at all times like its Head - it is inconceivable for it to be otherwise, for it was created in Christ.

We have shown the analogy before, how man and his complement, woman, should parallel the relationship that exists between Christ and His ecclesia (see the article, "The Origin of the Ecclesia" in Unsearchable Riches, Vol. 66, page 69). It should be clear in our minds that God gave a command to Adam to multiply and fill the earth, but Adam could not do this until his complement, woman, had been taken from him and presented to him. Then he was able to fulfil God's intentions through the one who was his complement, and ever since then generations of women have maintained "the form of humanity" as originally created by God in Adam. (Note, the original creation of humanity incorporated both sexes - see Genesis 1:27 and 5:2).

In exactly the same way, God's oath to Himself that He would be the only Saviour and that He would not rest until every knee should be bowing to Him, and every tongue acclaiming Him (Isa.45:22,23) - this could only be fulfilled through the One Who is His Complement - Christ. That is why Christ, as well as God Himself, is called the Saviour. In Titus 2, both God and Christ are referred to by this term, in verses 10 and 13 respectively.

It is similar with regard to Christ and His complement, the ecclesia. Until His work on the cross was fulfilled the ecclesia was (figuratively speaking) latent in Christ. But, like Adam, the Lord went into a deep stupor (in His case, death), and from the time of His resurrection onward, the ecclesia became a separate entity, to be presented to Him as His complement just as the woman was presented to man in Eden. This is the meaning of Ephesians 5:23-32.

Christ gave His life for the whole world - indeed, for the whole universe - but in a very special sense He gave it for the ecclesia. For if Christ had not given Himself up for us, there would have been no ecclesia. This is a thought which should be very precious to us all. And equally precious should be the thought (most wonderful as it is) that, without the ecclesia, Christ could not fulfil the purpose of God. That is why God is to have such glory in the ecclesia as well as in Christ throughout all the generations of the eon of the eons. Amen!

We have indicated how woman, the complement of man, has throughout many generations maintained the form of humanity as first created by God. This was the role appointed for her, for the "seed of the woman" was to bruise the head of the serpent, and that Seed must be in the likeness of humanity. So, too, will the ecclesia, as the complement of Christ, maintain the form of the ministry ordained for it by God "before the eons began". For our calling is "in accord with His own purpose, and the grace which is given to us in Christ Jesus before eonian times" (2 Tim.1:9). It is the grace of God which is the basis of all the ministry of the ecclesia; its members will, in fact, display His grace "among the celestials" in the eons to come (Eph.2:7).

The role of the Ecclesia
in God's Purpose

But that passage in 2 Timothy 1:9 also refers to the fact that we have been saved, and the first chapter of Ephesians also speaks of our "having the deliverance through His blood, the forgiveness of offenses in accord with the riches of His grace, which He lavishes on us" (verses 7, 8). This brings out another, and quite different, aspect of the ecclesia. As members of that composite whole, the body of Christ, we are seen by God to be "holy and flawless", and this we have been "in His sight" since the moment of our choice in Christ before the disruption of the world. But as individuals, chosen out of humanity, and needing to be brought into Christ (Rom.6:3), matters are quite different.

As members of humanity, we once walked in offenses and sins among the sons of stubbornness and "behaved ourselves in the lusts of our flesh, doing the will of the flesh, and were, in our nature, children of indignation, even as the rest" (Eph.2:1-3). Why was this? Why were we, who were predesignated to be sons of God and participants in an allotment that is holy and flawless, ever permitted to walk in accord with the eon of this world, and even in accord with the chief of the jurisdiction of the air?

The answer lies in the fact that grace has two aspects. It is either an act producing happiness, or a benefit bestowed on one who deserves the opposite. In the first aspect, it is exemplified in Christ, for God "graces Him with the name that is above every name" (Phil.2:9). Even before this, while He was on earth, Jesus was "full of grace and truth" (John 1:14). But the second aspect of grace can only be displayed to the full by the members of the ecclesia, and for them to be able to display it, they must have deserved the opposite. Hence the reason for their being chosen from the sons of humanity.

It was necessary for the ecclesia to share the experience of humanity, even as it was necessary for Christ to do so, though the reasons are different. The complement cannot be greater than its Head. Christ came to be in the likeness of humanity in order that He might be able to condemn and crucify sin; the ecclesia came to be in the likeness of humanity in order that it might display grace.

The work of Christ, as God's Complement, is to implement the promise of life, made in Him before eonian times, and therefore before God's purpose of the eons went into operation (2 Tim.1:1; Titus 1:2). The work of the ecclesia, as the complement of Christ, is to display God's grace in accord with the gift of grace, which also precedes eonian times (2 Tim.1:9).

It is a tremendous thought that the ministry of the ecclesia, like that of the Lord Jesus Christ, was fully determined by God, and provision made for its accomplishment, before He put any other part of His purpose into operation. Indeed, these two ministries - that of Christ and that of the ecclesia, which is His body - are thus complementary to each other, and form the basis upon which God's whole purpose is established. That is why God will find glory in the ecclesia and in Christ Jesus for all the generations of the eon of the eons.

The work of Christ, as God's Complement, brings life and peace to the universe; the work of the ecclesia, as Christ's complement, is to bring about a gracious acceptance of what Christ has done. The ecclesia is the complement by which Christ is completing the All in all, and thus make the whole universe (which is being headed up in Him) a worthy habitation of God's Spirit. For if God is All in all, then every creature becomes part of His dwelling place in spirit.

The Glory of our Allotment in Christ

The prospect that lies before the ecclesia, in its being used so effectively to display His grace is one that can only fill us with amazement and wonder. Adjectives are quite inadequate to express the glory of it. How can it be considered even remotely possible that we, chosen from sinful humanity, can ever be for the laud of God's glory? Yet it is so, and we have a pre-expectancy in Christ (Eph.1:12).

And there is no possible way in which can be thwarted of our expectation, for the apostle (in verses 13 and 14) goes on to tell us that, once we hear the evangel of our salvation and believe it, we are sealed in Christ with the holy spirit of promise,

and this is an earnest, or a pledge in kind, to us
that the eventual enjoyment of our allotment is secure. It has already been procured, and the spirit of
promise seals it firmly against any attempt to deprive
us of it. This, again, is for the laud of God's glory.

Before we conclude this study, we hope to give further thought to the tremendous issues involved in the
expression "God's dwelling place, in spirit", into
which we are even now being built together. For the
moment, let us remind ourselves of the words of Paul
in Ephesians 1:15-23 (one of the two momentous prayers
in this epistle, the other being in chapter 3; verses
14-21). The apostle realized that we shall need all
the wisdom and understanding that our loving Father is
able to give us if we are to grasp and enjoy the
glories of the expectation that is ours. He prays
that "the God of our Lord Jesus Christ, the Father of
glory, may be giving you a spirit of wisdom and revelation in the realization of Him, the eyes of your
heart having been enlightened, for you to perceive
what is the expectation of His calling, and what the
riches of the glory of the enjoyment of His allotment
among the saints, and what the transcendent greatness
of His power for us who are believing...." Note again
the emphasis on believing; the epistle is for the
saints, who are also believers.

All that God is doing in regard to the ecclesia is
in accord with the tremendous power which He used in
rousing Christ from among the dead, and exalting Him
to a position of authority above all others in heaven
and earth, whether they be sovereignties, authorities,
powers or lordships - whatever they are, none are now
above Him, but rather He is over them - and it is in
this sovereign capacity that He is given to the ecclesia, which is His body, the complement by which He is
completing the All in all. Thus there is no power in
the universe which can prevent the ecclesia, operating
in the power of Christ, from carrying out its function
in the eons to come, or can deny God the glory which
He has purposed to obtain through its ministry.

God is dwelling in Christ and in the ecclesia to-day; when the work of the ecclesia is finished, He will be dwelling in all His creatures, for the All in all will be completed.

Chapter Fifteen

THE NEW HUMANITY

The phrase, "God's dwelling place, in spirit", occurs, as we have previously noted, in Paul's letter to the Ephesians, which at once puts it in a celestial context. (The Ephesian epistle is characterized by the fivefold use of the expression "among the celestials".) It comes at the very end of the second chapter, and immediately before the apostle's second prayer, which opens the third chapter. We remember, of course, that these divisions into chapters are no part of original inspiration, and therefore the two chapters in question run on, the one into the other, as is indicated by the words "on this behalf."

The second chapter of Ephesians truly and firmly defines the basis of the joint body referred to in the third chapter. This basis is the cross of Christ, which effectively kills all the enmity previously existent in the flesh. For in the flesh there is a barrier between those termed Israel and the nations. Let us note here and now that this barrier had been established by God. He it was Who had inaugurated the rite of circumcision and had insisted upon it being carried out by those who were His people.

This rite was originally introduced to teach the lesson that the flesh was unable of itself to produce the result which God desired, and a small portion was to be cut off and cast away as a demonstration of the impotence of the rest. But Israel did not see it that way; to them it was a badge of distinction which separated them from other peoples. It is ever thus: the flesh cannot grasp the spiritual meaning of that which is of God, and it is in the inability of the flesh to do this that existent enmity is further provoked. The flesh even glorifies its own mutilation rather than admit its impotence.

This barrier between Israel and the nations was so firmly established and so clear cut that, not only did it confer on the former privileges denied to the latter, but it even made God "holy" (i.e., "wholly") to

160

Israel while excluding Him from the nations. To Israel God said, "You only have I known of all the families of the earth" (Amos 3:2), while of the nations it is written that they were "without God in the world" (Eph.2:12).

Thus, while ever this fleshly distinction lasted, God could not dwell among mankind as a whole; He must confine His presence to the nation of His choice.

Christ in Flesh
The Servant of the Circumcision

It was also true of Jesus that He was partial in His fleshly ministry. According to flesh, He was of the seed of David (Rom.1:3). He was not commissioned to serve any except the "lost sheep of the house of Israel" (Matt.15:24), and His disciples were equally restricted in their commission (Matt.10:5,6). He Himself was circumcised (Luke 2:21) and thus became identified with the Circumcision. As Paul says, in Romans 15:8, "Christ has become the Servant of the Circumcision, for the sake of the truth of God, to confirm the patriarchal promises."

The promises made to Abraham, Isaac and Jacob had been that their seed should be made into a great nation, and this was confirmed by God at Sinai, when He had declared that, if they obeyed His voice and kept His covenant, they should be a peculiar treasure unto Him above all people, for all the earth was His (Ex.19:5). There was thus an enmity in Christ's flesh towards the nations outside Israel, in that, in His flesh, He was bound to favour the people of God's choice, but this enmity (figured by the central wall of the barrier, which forbade people outside of Israel to enter the sacred places under pain of death) is completely eliminated at the cross (Eph.2:13-17). There a new humanity is created in Christ - a humanity which recognizes no fleshly distinctions, but one in which each of the former elements of mankind has equal right of access to the Father. Moreover, this is an unrestricted access, something which neither party had enjoyed before. The nations had had no access, Israel only a limited access in the person of their chief priest once every year.

In 2 Corinthians 5:16, Paul tells us that "we, from now on, are acquainted with no one according to flesh" and adds that "even if we have known Christ according to flesh, nevertheless now we know Him so no longer". If we were to continue to recognize Christ according to flesh, we should still be faced with that enmity in His flesh, which requires Him to be the Servant of Israel only and to exalt that nation above all others.

Here, in Ephesians, Christ is portrayed as the Head of a new humanity, which is not in accord with Adam, but in accord with God, and which is being created in righteousness and benignity of the truth (Eph.4:24). In this new humanity, there are none of the distinctions pertaining to the old humanity, for in it there is "no Greek and Jew, Circumcision and Uncircumcision, barbarian, Scythian, slave, free man, but all and in all is Christ" (Col.3:10,11).

What is Humanity?

Perhaps at this point we should pause to ask ourselves, "What is humanity?" This may seem a peculiar, if not a superfluous, question to raise, seeing that we are all members of humanity. Nevertheless, we still persist in asking it, since we feel that few are really clear in their understanding of what humanity actually is, and why it has come into being.

The first occurrence of the word "humanity" is significant in establishing its meaning. This is in Genesis 1:26 which reads, "And saying is Alueim, 'Make will We humanity in Our image, and according to Our likeness....'"

Let us put aside for a moment all thoughts of flesh and bones, of man being made from the soil of the ground, or of him being soulish (these details have their place in the second chapter of Genesis), and confine ourselves to the basic facts of the first chapter. Here the fundamental issue is that humanity was to be made in the image and likeness of its Creator. This is the prime concept which we should ever keep in mind when we are considering humanity. The fact that the word "create" is used no less than three times in verse 27 shows the importance of this development in God's operations, and shows, too, that nothing like this had ever been done before.

Celestial beings (excluding, of course, the Lord Himself) had not been created in the image of God, nor had the animals, though the introduction of soul life among creatures lower than humanity had also been a special creation (see Gen.1:21). But humanity was given extra glory and honour by being created in the image and likeness of God.

So that no one may be in any doubt, the basic truth of Genesis 1:27 is repeated in Genesis 5:1. Moreover, it is not annulled by man's original disobedience, or by any later consequences of this, for after a judgement which had destroyed all mankind (save for eight souls), we read in Genesis 9:6, "The shedder of the blood of a human, by a human his blood shall be shed, for in the image of Alueim has He made humanity."

We have thus established that humanity is a special creation, distinct from all else by its being in the image and likeness of God. Because of this, Christ (as God's true Image) could come to be in the likeness of humanity yet still be able to mirror the Father (John 14:9). And, to take the matter a little further, the ecclesia, which is the body of Christ, does not find its status jeopardized by its members being chosen from out of humanity, since humanity itself was created in the image and likeness of God.

Alas that that image has become sadly marred as a result of Adam's and subsequent transgressions, so tarnished and dulled that in humanity as a whole it no longer reflects the glory of God (Romans 3:23). Nevertheless, in spite of the blurring of its appearance, the form of humanity has not changed through numerous generations, for Jesus, when He became flesh, could truly be said to be "found in fashion as a man" (Phil. 2:8; Matt.16:16; John 1:49). And we, too, can become sons of God, and reflect His image while in the form of humanity, though this will only be true as we regard the old humanity as being "crucified together with Christ", and put on the new in its place (Rom. 6:6; Eph.4:24).

The Soulish and the Spiritual

The second chapter of Genesis describes how God formed a human out of the soil of the ground, and made him into a living soul by "blowing into his nostrils the breath of the living". Thus the first man was made both soilish and soulish, so taking on the characteristics described by Paul in 1 Corinthians 15, beginning at the middle of verse 44, to verse 49.

"If there is a soulish body, there is a spiritual also. Thus it is written also, The first man, Adam 'became a living soul'; the last Adam a vivifying Spirit. But not first the spiritual, but the soulish, thereupon the spiritual. The first man was out of the earth, soilish; the second Man is the Lord out of Heaven. Such as the soilish one is, such are those also who are soilish, and such as the Celestial One, such are those who are celestials. And according as we wear the image of the soilish, we should be wearing the image also of the Celestial."

"Not first the spiritual, but the soulish". This again is a profound truth. It implies that the spiritual could not be fully appreciated without first an experience of the soulish. When we suffer the infirmities of the soulish, we should bear this great fact in mind.

That which came to be known as the old humanity was soulish, and because of its soulish tendencies, soon became marred in the hands of the Divine Potter. It is a fundamental divine principle that God never mends that which has become marred, but always makes it anew. Hence there is no future for the old humanity. Like the marred vessel in the potter's hand (Jer. 18:4), the old humanity is crushed out of existence, but out of the same lump is created a new humanity, bearing none of the marred features of the old, but retaining its likeness to God. The old humanity was created in Adam, the new humanity is being created in Christ. The old was soulish; the new is spiritual. The head of the first was of the earth, soilish: the Head of the second is the Lord from heaven.

The old humanity is portrayed as being crucified together with Christ (Rom.6:6). It remains crucified for ever, that the body of Sin may be nullified. Though Christ Himself is resurrected, there is no resurrection for the old humanity. Instead it is replaced by a new (young) humanity, whose Head is Christ (not Adam), and in Christ there is "no Jew nor yet Greek... no slave nor yet free... no male and female, for you are all one in Christ Jesus" (Gal.3:28). There is thus a complete rift between the old and the new; in no sense is the latter a development of the former. "If anyone is in Christ, there is a new creation: the primitive passed by. Lo! there has come new" (2 Cor. 5:17).

Thus we see that the two humanities, old and new, meet in Christ. As the Seed of the woman, Christ took the old humanity with Him on to the cross, and it was crucified with Him. With His rousing from among the dead, He starts the new humanity, through which God will achieve all that He purposed when He first created humanity in His own image and likeness.

The Jurisdiction of Humanity

But in what sense is humanity in the image and likeness of God? When God declared His intention to so make humanity, He explained what His new creation was expected to do, namely to have "sway over the fish of the sea, the flyer of the heavens, and over the beast, and over all land life, and over every moving animal moving on the land" (Gen.1:26,28). Thus Adam was given dominion over the earth and over everything on earth that was of a lower order of creation than himself. In this respect he portrayed God and displayed His image. All that the animals could know about God was what they could see in humanity. This jurisdiction of humanity over the lower orders was confirmed when God brought every creature to Adam to be named and immediately endorsed the names which Adam gave them (Gen.2:19).

This jurisdiction was further confirmed in Psalm 8, where, after posing the question, "What is man?" David says, "All dost Thou set under his feet", and then elaborates this by adding, "Flocks and domestic animals, all of them, and even the beasts of the field; the birds of the heavens and the fish of the sea."

But when the writer of Hebrews quotes from this Psalm, and gives his response to this question he says simply, "Thou dost place him over the works of Thy hands. All dost Thou subject under his feet". (Heb. 2:7,8).

David defined that which was made subject to man, namely, domestic animals, beasts of the field, birds and fish. The writer of Hebrews omits this definition, for he wants to stress a different point. All was to be subject to humanity; nothing was to be left unsubject to him.

In the context of the old humanity, confined as it is by flesh and blood, it is obvious that this subjection must be limited to the lower creation. One of the reasons for the creation of the animals, birds and fishes was that the lesson of subjection should be taught. God Himself is a Subjector and Disposer, and Adam was made in the image and likeness of God that he might likewise be a subjector and disposer towards those placed under him.

In the context of the new humanity, that subjection is widened, and Christ (in Whom the new humanity has its origin) is presented to His ecclesia as Head over all, and that all includes the sovereignties, authorities, powers and lordships in heaven as well as on earth.

The Purpose of God in Humanity

God's purpose in creating humanity was to effect the salvation and ultimate reconciliation of all. At the time of its creation, a whole eon had elapsed, during which God's purpose concerned only celestial beings. Rebellion among these higher creations had taken place, and must have been of great magnitude to bring about the event known as the disruption. It was a disruption of the kosmos, or system, obtaining at that time. Its effects spilled over into the earth, causing chaos and vacancy and darkness. The evidences of disorder on this planet were indicative of the spiritual chaos which must have pervaded the heavens. To an outside observer, if there could have been one, it would have appeared as though God's purpose had ended in utter ruin.

But no, for before the disruption God had made provision for a Saviour (1 Peter 1:20), Who would give Himself for the universe. That One must of necessity be the One through Whom all else had been created, otherwise there might be some left out of His rescue work. The Firstborn of every creature must become the Firstborn from among the dead. But how was this One to die? Only by assuming a form in which death could operate. But this form had to be created, hence the need for humanity.*

But was the purpose of God in creating humanity completed in the cross? Was humanity created simply in order to provide a form in which Christ could come, and then be discarded as something that was of no further use? Thanks be to God that this is not the case.

God's Purpose Fulfilled in the New Humanity

God does not discard any of His creatures once they have served His purpose. If only we could begin all our considerations of God's Word with this profound truth in our minds, how different would be our thinking in many matters!

---

* See our booklet, "The Place of Humanity in God's Purpose" for further development of this theme.

Sinful humanity crucified the Son of God, and thereby ensured its own destruction. But humanity itself is not abandoned at the cross. It is the old humanity which is crucified there. The basic conception of humanity - a creation in the image and likeness of God - is carried through into the new humanity. The old humanity was "corrupting in accord with its seductive desires"; the new humanity is "in accord with God" and is being created in "righteousness and benignity of the truth" (Eph.4:22-24).

Through the old humanity the death of Christ was accomplished; through the new humanity, the reconciliation of all will be effected. For it is in the ecclesia (chosen out of humanity), as well as in Christ Jesus, Who came to be in the likeness of humanity, that God is to find glory throughout all the generations of the eons of the eons (Eph.3:21).

Humanity is thus the vehicle through which God accomplishes all, yet not in its own power but in His, and not in the way that humanity decrees, but in the way that God determines. His thoughts are not our thoughts, neither are His ways our ways. He can make the fury of men to acclaim Him. And even as He could use the sacrifices of animals to portray the supreme sacrifice of Christ, so He can use the "inferior" creation of humanity to point the way of reconciliation to those in the celestial realms. For do we not read that, through the ecclesia, the multifarious wisdom of God is being made known to even the sovereignties and authorities among the celestials - that is, to the highest in the heavenly hierarchy (Eph.3:10)?

It is God's purpose to "head up all in the Christ, both that in the heavens and that on the earth - in Him in Whom our lot is cast also" (Eph.1:10,11).

We inferred earlier that the spiritual could not be fully appreciated without first an experience of the soulish. This is true, not just for those who once were soulish, but also for those in the celestials who are continuously watching what is happening on earth. The soulish nature is intrinsically at enmity with God; it is not capable of pleasing Him. Nor without

the restraints imposed by His Spirit can it avoid
sinking further and further into depravity. Its culminating offense was in crucifying the Son of God, an
act calculated to bring the whole of the universe into
chaos (though men would be unaware of this), seeing
that it is in God's Son that all has its cohesion
(Col.1:17). What must the celestials have thought
when they witnessed this event? Did they see it as an
absolute and irreparable disaster? But the Firstborn
of every creature became the Firstborn from among the
dead, and the First of a new humanity, which, in accord with God, is being created in righteousness.
After Christ, the new humanity is represented in the
ecclesia, which is His body; eventually it will include all mankind, for "as it was through one offense
for all mankind for condemnation, thus also it is
through one just award for all mankind for life's justifying. For even as, through the disobedience of the
one man, the many were constituted sinners, thus also,
through the obedience of the One, the many shall be
constituted just" (Rom.5:18,19).

The old humanity is a demonstration to the universe
of the extent to which rebellion against God can lead;
the new humanity is a display to all of how God's
grace can operate to bring creation back into harmony
with Himself. The ecclesia is the advance instalment
of this new humanity, and is God's achievement at the
present time (Eph.2:10). Eventually all humanity will
be seen to be God's achievement, for He will personally wipe away all tears from their eyes, and will
tabernacle with them (Rev.21:3,4). And the celestials, too, having learned of His grace through the
ecclesia and having perceived God's kindness to those
who were once "children of indignation, even as the
rest", will also become His achievement.

Soulish humanity will have brought home to all the
lesson of sin, with its frightful consequences. From
the new spiritual humanity, all creation will receive
instruction in the ways of righteousness. And when
God's dealings with humanity, both old and new, are
truly assessed, there will grow in all such an en-

hanced appreciation of His love as to awaken in them a true realization of Himself, which He so desires, and a devout longing to reciprocate His love, which will fulfil His heart's delight.

In such an atmosphere as this does God find His true dwelling place in spirit; first in His Son, then in the ecclesia, and ultimately in all, for at the consummation He must be All in all.

Chapter Sixteen

BREADTH AND LENGTH
AND DEPTH AND HEIGHT

That God longs for a dwelling place among His creation has been made abundantly evident. It is natural
that humanity, created in His own image and likeness,
and Israel in particular, as His chosen people, should
desire to provide Him with such a dwelling place. We
saw this desire expressed in the song of Moses after
the deliverance from Egypt (Ex.15:2). But what humanity did not realize was its own inability to provide a
suitable habitation. God made it quite clear, in His
instructions to Moses regarding the details of the
original tabernacle and in His subsequent instructions
to David regarding the building of the temple, that He
alone was to determine the design of such a dwelling
place.

Moreover, even with such a dwelling place in the
midst of His people, access to His presence was se-
verely restricted, owing to the necessity of keeping
out that which was unholy. There was ever the threat
of destruction hanging over those who violated the
conditions of access. Clearly this could not be a
final solution.

Equally clearly, the final solution could not be
attained until all the spiritual barriers between God
and His creation had been removed. Hence, all the
ritual and sacrifices connected with the tabernacle
and the temple pointed to the supreme Offering and
Sacrifice made at Golgotha, where the One not knowing
sin was made to be sin, that sin itself could be
effectively destroyed.

The cross of Christ thus becomes the focal point of
God's purpose, for here Christ, as Chief Priest, offered Himself as a sacrifice without spot or blemish
for the whole of creation, of which He had been the
Firstborn. After His resurrection, He ascended into
the holy of holies, even heaven itself, in order to

place His offering before His God and Father, and to present Himself as the Firstfruits of the new humanity. Then He returned to earth with the assurance that access to God's presence was established.

Before He ascended to heaven the first time, Jesus knew that His offering would be accepted. He knew it even while He was on the cross, by the fact that the light returned after three hours of darkness. With the return of the light, signifying the ending of God's turning from Him, He was able to declare, "It is accomplished". The rending of the veil in the temple, from top to bottom, at the moment of His expiring, was God's indication that the way of access to His presence was now opened.

God is now Conciliated

That is why our message today is one of conciliation. God is conciliated to the world (kosmos) through the death of His Son. We should be beseeching, "For Christ's sake, be conciliated to God" (2 Cor.5:20). Christ went through all the harrowing experience of Golgotha to secure God's conciliation; for His sake, then, accept the friendship offered, and be conciliated to God. In other words, accept the preaching of the cross.

With the barrier of access to the Father removed, the way was opened for the presence and development of the ecclesia which is the body of Christ. But first the kingdom was reoffered to Israel, who showed their rejection of it by the stoning of Stephen. The immediate effect of the conciliation was to be seen in the call of Saul of Tarsus, who had officiated at this stoning. God was not holding any offense against him, but was choosing an enemy to be the official advocate of this new attitude. Saul was not only the first recipient of absolute grace, but, as Paul the apostle, became the chief announcer of it (1 Tim.1:11-16; Eph. 3:7,8; Col.1:25-29).

When Paul wrote his early letters to the Corinthians, humanity was divided into three classes. To

172

the Jews, absorbed in their religious practices, the word of the cross was a stumbling block. To the worldly wise, represented by the Greeks, the word was stupidity, since it did not accord with any of their philosophies. But to the third class, those who are saved, the word of the cross is the power of God and the wisdom of God, since in it they see coming into being a new humanity, headed up in Christ, which shall lead God's purpose into its glorious ultimate.

The ecclesia, which is Christ's body, is pre-expectant in the Christ. Through faith given to it by God (Eph.2:8; Rom.12:3), and by means of the indwelling influence of God's Spirit (Rom.8:9), we, its members, are able to perceive and appreciate the grace in which we are saved (Eph.2:8) and in which we now stand (Rom.5:2). With us, access to God becomes a reality (Eph.2:18 and 3:12); but note, this access is declared to be through Christ, Who is our Head. Through Him we can, even while still in flesh, pray direct to the Father, knowing that our prayers will be heard.

During this era of absolute grace, God is conciliated not just to the ecclesia, but to all. Not merely our fellow believers, but our friends and neighbours as well, and, indeed, our enemies too, benefit from the overflow of God's grace showered upon us. But once the ecclesia is taken out of the world, then God's indignation against all unrighteousness must be permitted to run its course, resulting in a time of tribulation of such intensity as has never been known before, nor ever will be experienced again (Matt. 24:21).

The Day of the Lord
and the Day of God

This time of tribulation ushers in the Day of the Lord, the millennial reign of Christ, with its restoration of the temple ritual (as outlined in Ezekiel's prophecy), all of which will be leading Israel to an acceptance of the truths contained in the book of Hebrews - a book which portrays the glories of

173

Christ's priesthood according to the order of Melchizedek.

We should never minimize these glories, nor those of His kingly rule. Together they will be greater than anything ever seen on earth before, and will indeed be the means of "leading many sons into glory" (Heb.2:10). Through this kingly priesthood, in which Israel will be participants, they will learn the value and efficacy of Christ's sacrifice, and will be brought to the position where they will be able to accept the preaching of the cross (at present anathema to them, and therefore a stumbling block), and enter into the joys of the new creation, as represented by the new heavens and new earth of Revelation 21.

In passing, it is instructive to note the consistency of the holy Spirit, in that the word "create" is not used in Revelation, for it is a book which stops short of proclaiming the word of the cross, a doctrine preached only by Paul. John, in Revelation 21:5, is inspired to use the word "make" of Isaiah 66:22 rather than the word "create" of Isaiah 65:17. Nevertheless, the latter scripture shows that the new heaven and the new earth are indeed a new creation.

The millennial eon, however, ends with a colossal rebellion on the part of humanity in general, as we read in Revelation 20, verses 7-9. This is followed by the judgement before the great white throne, in which those who have relied upon acts to justify them, are finally, but not irrevocably, condemned. For eventually (and in all our considerations of God's purpose, we must have the ultimate in mind) - eventually all who have died in Adam will be vivified in Christ, and God Himself will be All in all. Though the Scriptures do not actually speak (in so many words) of a resurrection from the second death, the wider implications of the two passages just referred to, in 1 Corinthians 15, as well as that in Colossians 1:20, certainly require it. In fact, they require no less than the vivification of all.

Meanwhile, in the last eon, the day of God, which follows the judgement of the great white throne, God

174

will be dwelling with all mankind (Rev.21:3). The passage reads, "And I hear a loud voice out of the throne saying, 'Lo! the tabernacle of God is with mankind, and He will be tabernacling with them, and they will be His peoples, and God Himself will be with them.'" The use of the word "tabernacle" indicates that this is not the final state. Just as the tabernacle in the wilderness gave way to something more permanent when the Israelites became settled in the land and the kingdom was established, and just as the patriarchs dwelt in tabernacles while they looked forward to the erection of something more permanent (Heb. 11:9,10), so God tabernacles with mankind (not just with Israel, but with all mankind) until the kingdom is completed, headed up in Christ, and is handed back to God. Then God will dwell, not with, but in, all His creation.

The Special Status of the Ecclesia

But now, in this interim period of absolute grace, we have a situation in which the joys of the ultimate are already being demonstrated. For even now God dwells in the heart of His Son (as, indeed, He always has done), and He also dwells in the hearts of those who are His. Both individually, and collectively, the members of the ecclesia are temples of God.

Figuratively speaking, God has always dwelt in the ecclesia as a whole, for it was chosen in Christ before the disruption of the world, that is, before anything happened to suggest that a barrier had arisen between God and any of His creatures. The ecclesia is (collectively) always "holy and flawless in His sight". Not only is it said to be chosen in Christ before the disruption, but it was (again figuratively speaking) latent in Him before even the eons began (2 Tim.1:9), and therefore before God's purpose of the eons was put into operation. But God can dwell in the hearts of individual members who are His and who put off the old humanity and put on the new, for the old humanity is irrevocably marred by sin, whilst the new

175

is guaranteed continuous perfection through its association with Christ.

The new humanity, as we saw in the last chapter, is a new creation, which can only be enjoyed after the old has been "passed by" - disposed of on the cross (Rom.6:6). Hence there is no point in proclaiming the new humanity unless the preaching of the cross has been made first, and this is done only in the writings of Paul. Nowhere outside of his writings are the values of the cross appreciated. That is why Paul carries us so much further than the other writers of Scripture, for without the preaching of the cross the purpose of God cannot be consummated. Paul completes the Word of God in every sense.

In similar fashion, the ecclesia, which is the body of Christ, completes the purpose of God. It is the medium through which Christ will complete the all in all (Eph.1:23). Without the ministry of the ecclesia the purpose of God again cannot be consummated; that is why God is to find "glory in the ecclesia and in Christ Jesus for all the generations of the eon of the eons" (Eph.3:21). It is for this that the ecclesia is pre-expectant in the Christ, its lot being cast in Him (Eph.1:11) and its life hidden together with Christ in God (Col.3:3).

A Holy Temple in the Lord

We now come to the wonderful passage in Ephesians 2, beginning at verse 19. In the previous verses (13-18), the barrier between Israel and the nations, existent in the old humanity, is broken down, and the verses conclude by stating that, through Christ, both those, who were formerly afar off, and those who were near, are given the same privilege of access, in one spirit, to the Father. This is an unrestricted access, far superior to anything ever enjoyed by Israel, the favoured nation, in the past.

None in the ecclesia are now guests and sojourners (as they were before the barrier was removed), but all are fellow-citizens of the saints, and all are said to belong to God's **family**. This is the only occasion that this last word is used in Scripture in connection with God. It comes from a root word (oikos) meaning "home". This is a family where each is at home with the others - not a family which is scattered, as earthly families often are. In particular, God desires and determines to make His home within this family, which is being built on the foundation of the apostles and prophets. Notice how the metaphor is abruptly changed from a family to a building: "... being **built** on the **foundation** of the apostles and prophets, the **capstone of the corner** being Christ Jesus Himself, in Whom the **entire building**, being **connected together** [with the mortar of God's Spirit] is growing into a **holy temple** in the Lord; in Whom you, also, are being **built together** for God's **dwelling place**, in spirit."

The whole of God's purpose concerning His Son and concerning creation has been conceived, and put into operation, with the aim of achieving this result, namely, the building of a spiritual, holy temple, in which every kindred in the heavens and on earth is to be incorporated (Eph.3:15), and of which we, the ecclesia, are the prior and prime instalment. It is the acme of God's desire, the pinnacle of His delight, the apex of His achievements - to have every kindred in heaven and earth **named in Himself**, that is, acknowledging Him as **Father**. Already the ecclesia acknowledges Him as both God and Father (1 Cor.8:6), but that perception is still far away from the rest of creation, and a lot of work has to be done through the medium of the ecclesia before creation as a whole comes into a full realization of God. But Paul's prayer, in Ephesians 3, verses 14-21, is for the ecclesia itself to have sufficient staunchness of faith to be able to grasp the tremendous dimensions - the breadth and length and depth and height - of the ministry for which it has been chosen, called and prepared.

The foundation of this ministry, as with all God's operations, is love - the love which could not be contained within the bosom of the Father, but needed to burst forth for the blessing of all His creatures. And how the Father has waited for that love to be reciprocated! Not in the case of His Son, for there the love of God found an immediate and everlasting response. But in our case, the response is tardy and inadequate - hence the need for the apostle's prayers. We should sharpen our responses to accord with the tremendous favours which are being lavished upon us, the riches of His grace (Eph.1:8).

Through the ecclesia, God is to display the transcendent riches of His grace in the oncoming eons, to the end that all may eventually grow into this holy temple in the Lord. The two Ephesian prayers of Paul are uttered with the desire and intent that we, as members of that ecclesia, should recognize (1) the nature of our calling, and its ultimate aim; (2) the riches of its glory; and (3) the transcendent greatness of the power operating on our behalf until that ultimate is attained. We are being completed for the entire complement of God; through us He is completing the all in all.

Breadth and Length and Depth and Height

In his pamphlet, "Breadth and Length and Depth and Height", Brother E. H. Clayton writes of these four terms of extension: "Do they not figure the grandeur of God's dwelling place to which the saints are thus connected, and also intimate the inclusiveness of the ultimate results to God? Truly we are for the outcome of His transcendent love. The fruit of this economy, distinct as it is, is not merely for our blessing, but for God's glory in the universe. This achievement God is fashioning by His power directed by His love."

"The measurements of the physical dwelling places of God - the tabernacle, the temples, and also the holy city, are all given in finite terms, and are confined to breadth, length and height. Here, in describing this spiritual dwelling place of God, a fourth dimension is added. In no direction can we go to find exclusion from this dwelling place, nor is there any distance to which we can go to escape from it, since all the dimensions are now infinite - without any limits whatsoever. Not that any of God's creatures will wish to escape from His all-embracing love, for God's homing in each and all will bring them joy and gladness beyond measure, and fulfil the desires of their hearts as well as His."

The Ultimate Attainment:
God's Dwelling Place in Spirit

The ecclesia, which is Christ's body, is His complement by which the whole universe is to be served, and through which all in heaven and earth are to receive the blessings of the conciliation. In the glory of the new creation, and in the righteousness of the new humanity, the ecclesia will be functioning to display God's grace to all, and all will come to realize the vastness of His love, and share in the right of access to His presence. The power that is, and will be, operating in the ecclesia is from the One Who is able to do superexcessively above all that we are requesting or apprehending, but it is a power that God will delight to employ to the uttermost, for it will bring glory to Himself throughout all the generations of the eon of the eons, and completely satisfying blessings to all His creatures.

In some notes on "God's Dwelling Place" (from which we quoted in an earlier chapter, and we cannot do better than to quote further), Brother Alan Reid writes,

"Staunchness with power and strength rooted and grounded in love to grasp the dimensions of God's dwelling place in spirit, are indeed required by each member of the ecclesia which is the body of Christ and His complement, for this is the ultimate which will embrace every kindred in the heavens and on the earth. There is an inclusiveness expressed in the terms used - every kindred, entire building and entire complement - that compasses not only the creatures of the earth, but also of the heavens. All is to be headed up in

179

Christ, both in the heavens and on the earth (Eph. 1:10).

"This is greater by far than the Israel of God and greater than the ecclesia within whose individual members God's Spirit now makes its home. This views even a wider range than God's tabernacling with mankind in the new earth. This is the **reconciliation of the all through Christ**, - whether those on the **earth** or those in the **heavens** (Col.1:20). **This is God All in all** (1 Cor.15:28), **God's dwelling place in all, in spirit**."

This is the goal of God's desires, in which is perceived the glory of His achievements, and the reason for all His operations in the furtherance of His purpose. This is all we know, and all we need to know, for this is the topmost pinnacle of Divine revelation.

*****